Published by Over And Above

Editor: Rick Benzel
Cover and Book Design: Susan Shankin
Over and Above Creative Group, Los ᷄
www.overandabovecreative.c

CW00923471

Copyright © 2015 by Marc Koehler. All rights reserved. This book contains material protected under International and Federal Copyright Laws and Treaties. No part of this publication may be reproduced, distributed, or transmitted in any form or by any means, including photocopying, recording, or other electronic or mechanical methods, without the prior written permission of the author, except in the case of brief quotations embodied in critical reviews and certain other noncommercial uses permitted by copyright law. For permission requests, please email the author at following address: Marc@LeadWithPurpose.com

Library of Congress Control Number: 2015936254
ISBN: 978-0-9907924-4-4

Visit our website and blog for updates: ww.LeadWithPurpose.com

To the people who matter the most to me, thanks to my wife Heidi and my children Anja, Liesel, and Sophie who have taught me invaluable life lessons and allowed me to follow my passion.

I am truly blessed to have you in my life.

What CEOs and Executive Leaders Are Saying about *Leading With Purpose*

"We turned our stagnant 32-page plan in a binder into a living one-page plan that is managed online. Now every employee understands how their daily activities are linked to our higher goal and purpose. It provides us what we need to chart a course to achieve goals, gain alignment throughout our organization, and manage the ever-changing business environment."
—TODD MATTSON, *President and Owner, Pro-Line Racing Inc.*

"I used to feel the need to micromanage everyone's day. Now, I am out of the minutia because each person understands our long-term vision along with their top three goals. Employees are learning and growing, and I have more time to spend leading the business."
—GREGG SCHNEIDER, *CEO, Caseworx Inc.*

"For years I read every book and attended every leadership seminar, but saw little progress in aligning my staff and strengthening my company. With this book, my team was able to develop a clear plan that they took ownership of and within 6 weeks, I saw real results. Most importantly, I now truly feel like a CEO."
—DREW LOUIS, *CEO, Owner, Del Toro Loan Servicing*

"*Leading With Purpose* helped me take the passion in my heart and the vision in my head and create a simple story for my employees who are now more passionate and focused. I don't feel alone anymore and it is now a true team effort with everyone on the same page."
—BOB FELIX, *Owner and President, AAP Inc.*

"*Leading With Purpose* made it possible for my team to have a say in who we are, what we believe in, and what needs to get done. This has bonded us in a new way and is helping us to build this dream of ours. After 8 years in business, I finally have everyone on the same page rowing in the same direction."
—RON COTTRELL, *President/Owner Active Mobility*

"The number one challenge I have as a business coach is helping 25 CEO's and business owners stay focused. Distractions and urgencies lure them away from leading their companies. *Leading With Purpose* helps me focus them—simply—on the most important goals that align with their company's mission and values. It is in a format that everyone in their company can easily read and understand."
—JOE LARUSSA, *Convene Chair, Executive Coach to 25 Business Owners*

"Ten years from now I will be telling people how monumental *Leading With Purpose* was to our business and how it shaped what we have become."
— JON KRYSTAFIK, *Business Manager, Safeway BSI Inc.*

"Each year our company chooses one book for all the managers to read before our annual meeting. Past choices have been *From Good to Great* and *Flawless Execution*. This year, I am recommending Marc Koehler's book. I was even inspired to adapt his techniques to my marriage and family planning."
—TERRY MADDUX, *Training Manager, ShopFreedom.com*

"For the last 15 years, I have had a vision of where I wanted to take the company. *Leading With Purpose* helped me finally to crystallize it succinctly so everyone else understands it also."
—DAVE TRIEPKE, *President, Universal Metro, Inc.*

"I would recommend *Leading With Purpose* to anyone serious about designing the business of their dreams."
—CLAY CONNER, *President, The Conner Group*

"This easy-to-understand book would benefit any leader looking to take their business to the next level. I love the simplicity and powerful messages! "
—CATHY ELLIS, *President, Ellis and Associates*

"*Leading With Purpose* is a tremendous resource and helps our team focus on the most important elements of planning and sharing not only the vision, but also the specifics of the plan with all of our employees. We continue to benefit in our third year of using the tools and approach."

—STEW EDINGER, *Senior Vice President, Federal Heath*

"By establishing our purpose, declaring our values and creating a mission, we were able to establish goals and put effective management in place. The one-page plan puts everything at your finger-tips and best of all...it's cloud based so there is no looking for saved files or thumbing through binders. Thanks."
—LARRY NIELSEN, *Nielsen Marketing Services, President*

Foreword

If you have ever been frustrated at work because you didn't feel valued by your organization, or as its leader you were frustrated by the lack of passion, initiative, and creativity of your people—you are not alone.

Theoretically, organizational success should be simple. Leaders want organizations where people work with a unity of effort, everybody moving in the same direction. They also want to empower their people, by which I mean enable them to make decisions. Employees want the same things. They, too, want a sense of purpose and they want jobs where they can make meaningful decisions that contribute to helping others inside and outside the organization.

Unfortunately, we usually get one or the other, but not both: either we get unity of effort or distributed decision making. When push comes to shove, bosses would rather have unity of effort rather than empowerment. They enforce this by having everyone think and do as they're told.

At the core, leaders are often afraid that empowering their people will come at the cost of keeping everyone moving in the same direction, that "empowered" people will make decisions not aligned to the long-term goals of the organization.

There is a key to having both—and that key is in this book. That key is *purpose.* It's only when companies are clear about their purpose, have clearly communicated it, and it is understood by the team that companies can achieve both unity of effort and distributed decision making. The purpose statement can't be a lofty saying that sits in a frame mounted on the wall. That is not helpful. The purpose must be so clear that it helps the members of the organization in the day-to-day decision making on their jobs.

Marc and I share several similarities. For example, we both served on nuclear submarines; we both have had the opportunity to turn around failing organizations; we both have had to rethink what we "knew" about leadership; and we both have written books based on our experience.

But more important than all of those things, we both share a passion for creating a world where people can contribute so they feel valued; and since they feel valued, they contribute. It is a world where people show up at work with a sense of purpose and go home at the end of the day with a sense of accomplishment.

In this book, you will find ideas, practices, and tools that will help you join us on that journey.

—L. DAVID MARQUET, author of *Turn the Ship Around!: A True Story of Turning Followers into Leaders*, named #1 Must-Read Business Book of 2012 (Fortune) and 12 Best Business Books of all Time (Motley Fool)

Introduction

Helping People Lead a More Purposeful Life. This is our purpose. This is what drives us. This is what we are passionate about. Our company, Lead With Purpose, was born out of 30+ years of real-world experiences in business, family, and coaching leadership positions. If you are in a leadership position you certainly have a lot of authority and responsibility, but are you using the great opportunity you have to be a *leader* and help people lead more fulfilling and purposeful lives?

Our approach to leadership is grounded in three simple steps that any person can learn. The first is to *engage* people so they understand the difference they make in the world. The second step is to *empower* people to make decisions and take control of their goals and life. The final step is to *encourage* people as they travel on their journey. So whether you are the President of a fifty-person company, a parent to your children, or the head coach of the 9 year-old Yellow Dragons soccer team, you can use the *Engage, Empower,* and *Encourage* approach to help the people you lead reach their full potential.

Leading With Purpose is our first book and is focused on helping you as a business leader become more effective, empowering, and successful in every aspect of your work. It shows you how to envision a strong future for your company and provide caring and intelligent direction. While this book is focused on helping you to transform yourself and the people you lead in a business environment, our future books and programs will help you to parent or coach or pray with purpose. You can learn more by going to www.LeadWithPurpose.com.

***

Leading With Purpose

If you are the CEO or President of a small- to mid-sized company, are you struggling with one or more of the following challenges?

· Creating a clear, purposeful vision that guides your entire company.
• Finding dedicated employees who are passionate about your product or service and willing to work hard to help you succeed.
• Establishing meaningful goals that stretch people to achieve and make your company great.
• Keeping everyone focused on the key tasks and goals that contribute to your growth and success.
• Feeling that you need to micromanage every decision made at your company.
• Adapting quickly to change and adjusting your long- and short-term goals accordingly.
• Barely getting by and struggling to make a profit.
• Building your own leadership skills so you can evolve and improve as your company grows.

Leading With Purpose helps you meet these challenges and take your organization to a new level of excellence. This book increases your ability to attract the best employees—and keep them because you have won their hearts and minds. It shows you how to foster a highly engaged attitude from every employee in your company. It literally puts your entire team all on the same page, ensuring that everyone understands your mission, your values, your long-term goals and how their own accountabilities link to them. It allows you to empower your people and push decision making down to them. It can boost your revenues and add to your net profitability. And, most importantly, this book can help you become the leader you have always wanted to be: clear and committed to leading with purpose and focused on what matters most.

How does this book accomplish these goals? The answer: It teaches you how to craft your company's unique and inspiring story of the reason it exists and the difference it makes in the world along with the values and beliefs of your culture. Then, we show you how to create a set of aligned goals that cascade over different time horizons clearly revealing for everyone what they need to focus on today and how it is connected to the big picture vision. What is unique is that all of this information will sit on a single page. Yes, a single page! You won't need any staples, paperclips, or even a binder.

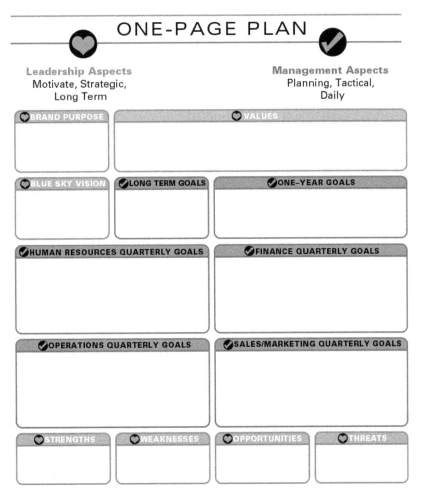

You and your team will produce your own one-page plan which will become the key to helping you meet today's leadership challenges of growing companies with high hopes. It is easy to use and serves as a North Star to guide you and everyone in your company. It combines the key elements of strategic thinking with setting goals that hold everyone accountable and organizes your planning and goal setting as you have never been able to do before. One of the most important benefits of your one-page plan is that it connects strategy to execution. It links the company's purpose, values, and vision directly to everyone's job.

I have used a one-page plan in scores of companies where I was brought in as an interim CEO to turn the firm around. In this role, I took full responsibility for operations, payroll, hiring, firing, and profitability as if the company were my own. I have saved numerous firms from bankruptcy or outright extinction using a one-page plan and the principles detailed in this book.

This is not complicated or difficult to implement. I know that many business executives would rather hide in a closet than think about "strategic planning" or creating accountability goals. For many leaders and managers, planning feels like a homework assignment, a chore, an inefficient time-consuming task that makes them want to avoid it.

But I assure you that the plan you create is built on simplicity and ease of use. The truth of this will be demonstrated the moment you begin using it. As a system, it makes so much sense that you won't find yourself resisting it. Your managers and employees will equally find it valuable and relevant to their work. All in all, a one-page plan is what you need to finally master the leadership challenges that interfere with your professional and personal success.

My Discovery of the One-Page Plan

I am an engineer with B.S. degrees in both physics and mechanical engineering, as well as rigorous training in nuclear engineering from the U.S. Navy that approximates a Master's degree. I served as a Lieutenant on the nuclear submarine USS Pogy SSN 647. My years in the Navy helped me develop a love for systems and for wanting to master the challenges of decision-making in large organizations. In the Navy, when we were circling the globe underwater without the ability to surface or communicate with our headquarters, we had our orders to follow—but we also had to make quick decisions with intelligence, confidence, and commitment. I credit the Navy with giving me an appreciation for top-notch leadership in organizations.

After my years on a sub, I returned to civilian life and went into business. I intended to use my naval leadership skills to help companies. I worked for Honeywell for several years. The training I received there in leadership, lean principles, and strategic planning was first class. I was a disciple of some of the great thinkers on leadership and management. One of my favorites was Jim Collins, author of *Good to Great*. I absorbed ideas from him and many other luminaries who wrote about leadership and building companies that survive change.

After Honeywell, I worked for smaller companies in operations roles. One of the skills I brought into my job was a strong eye for strategy and planning. At one company, I saw that employees were not engaged in their work because they didn't understand what their company was all about or what role they played in helping it achieve success. The company had no plan, so I took it upon myself and spent weeks on end, writing a lengthy strategic plan that ultimately brought the team together and guided the company towards profitability. It was exciting to see how my efforts motivated employees and impacted the company. Through this experience I discovered my passion for the strategic management side of business.

In 2005, I followed that passion and launched my own consulting firm, focused on providing strategic management and operations expertise. My first client was a small US-based manufacturing company. I became its interim COO and went in like a bull in a china shop, eager to use all my skills and experience. This firm had grown from 20 employees to 50 in just five years. Its founder and CEO was struggling to keep up with leading an organization where he no longer knew everyone and felt he had lost control. He hadn't changed his leadership style and didn't understand what he needed to do to be effective and regain his former momentum.

In my first few weeks on the job, I evaluated all of their systems and teams. When I asked the President to rate the management team, he said they were mediocre. When I asked him about making changes and bringing in better people, he became uncomfortable and asked me to try to make it work with the current group. Also, I discovered that the firm had no strategic plan. None, nada! No document spelled out the company's mission, vision, long-term objectives and short-term goals. A mediocre team with no plan. No wonder the company was flailing, or so I thought.

I spent the next six weeks leading the senior management team through powerful strategic planning exercises that I had learned during my years in the Navy, my training at Honeywell, and many great books I had read about strategic planning and management. I wanted the team to understand strategic planning as well as I did and how their jobs connected to the company's vision. I required everyone to read Jim Collin's *Good to Great* and I assigned articles from the Harvard Business Review.

I took the team on a 4–day offsite retreat where we met in a huge conference room with whiteboards, easel pads, and sticky notes. We did some "serious play" constructionist work using squishy toys and slinkies—all in an effort to spark their creativity and inspire new ideas for the company's direction. We did team building work, like falling backwards into each other's arms to build trust and camaraderie. Each night, we had fabulous dinners and sat around sharing ideas. Finally, we closed the retreat with an entire afternoon dedicated to writing a new mission statement. Everyone left feeling upbeat and jazzed. It seemed successful.

I went home believing that I had just helped the management team gain more clarity than they had ever had before. That week, I wrote a "brilliant" (or so I thought) 32 page master strategic plan. I printed it out and gave a binder to every leader who had been on the retreat. They dutifully read it and in our next weekly management meeting, I began asking the team about the plan to make sure they had studied and learned it. "Bill, what is our Vision?" I called out.

"Mary, what are our Values?" I was patient as the team stumbled through the exercise. The following week, I did it again, believing that practice would make perfect. By the third week, I was astonished when the team still couldn't answer the questions without fumbling over the words and making errors. I was feeling completely dejected. It seemed that little progress had been made in assimilating the plan into their hearts and minds.

I went home that weekend and was completely baffled. I looked over the strategic plan and compared it to others I had written for companies in the past. This plan seemed so straightforward—and it was only 32 pages. How hard could that be?

The following week, at our next management meeting, I leveled with the team. "Ok, what is going on here?" I asked. "Why aren't you all remembering the strategic plan that we spent 4 days working on?" No one replied at first.

Then one of the best managers in the company, a woman I'll call Lisa, raised her hand. What she said rocked my worldview. "Marc, over the past few months you've been here, you asked us to be frank with you. I learned a lot from you doing this strategic plan. We had a lot of fun as a team and we bonded more than ever before. I'm certain there is a lot of value in what we did, but I am back at work now." Then Lisa placed her hand on the binder, looked up at me and pointedly asked:

Marc, how does this help me do my job?

Her question caught me off guard. I stood there open mouthed, trying to formulate my answer. Then it dawned on me: if Lisa felt this way, maybe others did. I began asking the rest of the team what they thought about the strategic plan. To a person, they told me the same thing—the document just didn't help them do their jobs any differently from what they were already doing. One manager commented in a way that cut through powerfully to me. "Marc," he said, "it just feels like a never-ending high school homework assignment."

That was revealing. It told me the team could not identify with the plan's elements—really taking them to heart. The mission statement, vision, company values—all these were nothing but a jumble of paragraphs and words to them. While I was extremely proud of this masterpiece I had created, the team couldn't see how the contents translated into their real world. I looked at the plan in my hands and, noticing it filled a one-inch binder, I started to get an inkling of what was wrong.

Over the weekend, I wrestled with my theories about planning and leadership. I researched different ideas and re-read management books that had long been my favorites. I decided I needed to make a key change—the strategic plan had to be shorter, more succinct, and especially more memorable. I took my 32–page masterpiece and began extracting the most pertinent sections. I honed and whittled the wording down. I simplified key phrases. I used plain English.

The following Monday, I went into our weekly management meeting and presented the team with the new version—it was *just 7 pages long*. There were nods of approval all around.

Over the next few months, the management team digested and assimilated the shorter plan as never before. It was exciting. They became more engaged and started to go the extra mile in their jobs. With this new plan, they finally understood the company's reason for existence and their own role in making a difference. This team, which was quite mediocre before, led the company back to health and profitability—but more importantly, they taught me a huge lesson: *Keep it Simple, Short, and Clear*.

During the next seven years, I was brought into other distressed companies as interim CEO. I developed a reputation as someone who could tackle the worst situations—businesses that had lost their way and were failing. Many were on the verge of going under. In each experience, I continued to refine and test my newfound ideas about how to craft plans that have impact on people. I found that the key to my success had to do with shortening the plan more—and even more. My plans to rescue companies went from 7 pages, to 4 pages, to 3 pages, to 2 pages...*and finally to just a single page!*

It became clear to me that what I had discovered represented a whole new approach to leadership and management—combining the best aspects of strategic planning with operational goal setting and putting all of the results on a single page where *everyone* in the company can see it, learn it, and commit to achieving it.

What you are about to go through was borne out of my real experiences of turning around failing businesses. It is not based on theoretical concepts devised while standing on the sidelines. The success of the many turnarounds I led was directly linked to implementing a one-page plan in those companies. Even other advisors at the companies where I was working saw the impact of the plan and began using it in their own consulting practices.

Most recently, I have learned that several notable companies use similar short-style plans—and I consider this a strong confirmation of this approach. Ford Motor Company's CEO, for instance, uses a one-page document to keep track of the leading objectives for the company. The CEO of the online cloud storage site, Box, uses one sheet of paper listing the company's 50 top tasks to complete. My sense is that this is one of the next trends in leadership. Here's why.

Focusing on What Matters Most

Leaders want to know what they need to do and focus on so they can make their company stronger and more valuable. I am sure you have had these thoughts also. Creating a one-page plan and using the principles in this book is powerful because it helps company leaders *lead with purpose*, by which I mean that it helps them focus on what matters most.

So what matters most?

In my view, whether you are company with 30, 50, or 1000 employees, the most important factors to surviving and thriving in today's fast-paced, chaotic, global business world are these four:

- *Passion.* Companies need people at every level who are passionate about their work. Typically, a CEO founds a company because he or she is passionate about a product, service, or cause. This passion translates into a vision that inspires everyone. The most engaged managers and employees are those who love their jobs and share the vision of their leaders to ensure the company succeeds over the long term.

Passion drives them to be committed to their work, to go above and beyond their job description, to praise the company to outsiders, and to desire to stay at the company for years, if not forever. Passionate employees who understand the long-term vision more easily manage the short-term stresses and changes that inevitably occur.

• *Product.* A company must have a product or service that solves a problem that a lot of customers are willing to spend either time or money to use.

• *Productivity.* In today's world, if you are not productive, your competitors will surge ahead of you. A company's productivity is found in the quality of its tools, resources, and systems. It is also found in the creativity of its innovation and in the quantity of services or products it produces for its clients. Leaders who inspire their employees to be engaged in their jobs derive the most productivity. People become willing to go that extra mile to satisfy customers, help co-workers, or create new ideas that could help the organization.

• *Profit.* Companies that survive and thrive make a profit. This is the inescapable fact of business. Without a positive return on investment (ROI), the company cannot pay its employees, compensate stakeholders, or have the resources to continually invest in its own future. Profits enable a company to reward employees, grow their offerings, and expand their locations.

Although there may be other factors that are important to your individual company, these four elements are *what matter most* in keeping a company alive. The reason I was brought into so many distressed companies was almost always due to one or more of those four factors. Either employee passion was lagging or non-existent, or people didn't have all the tools or processes in place and were thus unproductive, or profitability was negative. As an interim CEO, I know from experience that companies that fail to prioritize these four factors in their planning and operations are very likely to experience problems soon.

My Journey from People to Passion

You may be surprised that the first factor is Passion. Before I started my first interim assignment, I would have also been surprised as I used to sequence the four factors that mattered most as follows: People, Product, Productivity, and Profits. In other words, for me, People was the first factor back then. *The strongest companies had the smartest and most talented group of employees who were committed to helping the company win.* It is important for you to fully understand this fundamental shift from People to Passion.

When I started my interim CEO work, my goal was to have a positive impact in as many of these four areas and turn the company back over to investors. My six- to nine-month vision would usually be based on helping the most talented group of people have all the tools they need to be productive. The company could then produce an exceptional product that customers valued. All of this contributed to a more profitable financial situation.

I soon learned that the challenges of being an interim CEO hampered that initial approach. You see, owners and Boards of Directors turn to outside interims when conditions have seriously deteriorated and several attempts to right the ship on their own have proven unsuccessful. They want answers in six weeks, not six months, and they don't want to invest more money until they know if there is a path back to success.

Not having a lot of time or money changed what I could do in all four areas of what matters most. I couldn't afford to hire the best people in the world, nor could I even entice them to leave their current job and come work for a company that might not be around in six months. I couldn't significantly change the product or invest in the latest manufacturing equipment that would make the company more productive.

In the first few weeks of a new assignment, I had my check list. It included asking lots of questions, evaluating current systems, reviewing financials, watching how the company operated, and completing a one-page plan. Although current management was failing in running the business, they had most of the answers needed to create such a plan. It was a simple process that helped me work with the team to create our unique story while uncovering the most pressing challenges. I used the plan as a roadmap to success for the management team, the employees, and Board of Directors.

I would then roll it out to the entire company. The plan was on a single page so it was easy for me to explain and easy for employees to understand. People left the rollout knowing the difference the company makes in the world, the company's current challenges, and what they needed to focus on today.

Over the next month, I carried the plan with me and referenced it in as many conversations as I could. *This is the difference we are making. These are our values. How are you coming along on your goals?* During this time, I noticed that some people were becoming more passionate about what they were doing. They had more energy and were more productive.

Oddly, it seemed that a one-page plan was solving the challenge of not being able to bring in the best people from the outside. I found that the existing employees were taking more ownership and going above and beyond. I was starting to see there was a different path to bolstering the People factor. The most talented employees are valuable, but employees who were passionate about what they are doing are just perhaps slightly more valuable.

My Study of What Inspires Humans

I became interested in understanding why these employees had been underperforming and what caused them to change into passionate, productive, and engaged people, interested in their company's success (i.e., its profitability). I began studying human nature in depth by asking employees deeply probing questions. *Do you like your job? What would motivate you to work hard? What goals do you have in your own career? What makes a company great to work for?*

I also studied the statistics and research on employee engagement —and I had a real awakening. The fact is, employee engagement is at record lows in U.S. companies both large and small. One of the most comprehensive studies of employee engagement comes from the Gallup organization, performed every two years.[1] In 2013, Gallup reported the following results about the entirety of the US workforce:

- *Actively Disengaged.* 20% of workers are miserable in their jobs. They hate their work and are actively looking for another job. They simply don't care about their company.

- *Not Engaged.* 50% of workers are apathetic about their jobs. They come to work dispassionate and disinterested in their company's success, checking in and out at the same time every day. They rarely make suggestions or go above and beyond what is minimally needed to get their work completed.

- *Engaged.* Only 30% love their job. Less than 1 in 3 employees say they are passionate about their work and are engaged in the company's efforts to succeed.

Think about these shocking statistics. Combining the miserable and apathetic groups, a whopping 70% of people working today are spending eight hours of every day not doing their best to fulfill their jobs. This is estimated to cost $500 billion in lost productivity in the U.S. alone. *That's a lot of businesses struggling with employee engagement.*

Two other studies support the need to boost employee engagement. A Harvard Business Review study found that 95% of people don't understand how they can help contribute to their company's strategic plan, suggesting that this is a huge problem for leadership.[2] Meanwhile, another Gallup survey showed that it pays to have highly engaged employees: companies in the top quartile of employee engagement are 22% more profitable than those in the bottom quartile.

During this time, two other leadership areas of my life contributed to my understanding of what inspires people. First, as a leader in my family, I was reading every book I could on how to be a better husband to my wife and father to my three young children, but that didn't prepare me for all the different situations I would encounter. Second, as a soccer coach of 8 to 10 year-old children, my leadership and communication skills were tested every time I stepped on to the field, not only teaching the children, but also managing many overzealous parents.

Every day, I was effectively submersed in a sort of "leadership boot camp." I would rise in the morning and help my kids prepare for the day. I then went to lead a distressed company, working with the management team and employees to help turn the business around. After work, I spent a couple of hours teaching young children how to play soccer. The nights were occupied with helping my kids with their homework and spending time with my wife. The weekends were a mix of catching up on business, family activities, and coaching soccer games. This was my weekly routine for seven years.

I learned a lot during that time, and the thousands of interactions I had in my life helped me look deeply into the hearts of human beings and see what inspires them. Whether it was in business, in my family, or on the soccer field, I was able to conclude these three principles about humans.

All humans:
• crave simple messages that are meaningful to their lives;
• want to belong to something bigger than themselves;
• get excited when they know they are making a difference to others in the world.

These three principles led me to conclude that one of the keys to effective leadership is inspiring people to be passionate about their work and believe their jobs make a difference in the world. Giving people positive feelings for the long days they spend in their jobs is how leaders generate engaged employees.

This is the moment when my understanding of which of the four factors that matters most changed. Rather than going out and "finding" the best people (a push strategy), leaders who create simple, meaningful messages will help bring out the best in every employee and also attract the best people from the outside (a pull strategy). Leaders who have vision and an inspiring story to tell are the ones with whom the "A players" want to work. Simply put, leaders with passion attract employees with passion to match.

Furthermore, when a company's vision is large and workers feel they are involved in something bigger than themselves and sense their jobs make a difference in the world, they will boost their own engagement. It doesn't matter what that "bigness" or meaning is about. It could be saving people's lives, producing dog food, cutting lumber, or bagging groceries—when people believe their work contributes to a higher purpose, they strive to do their best.

I came to recognize these principles of human nature just as I was developing the plan's format. Little by little, I incorporated my new understanding into its design and structure. Over the years of using our one-page plan in real companies, I have seen how it matches these principles of human nature better than other leadership tools. These experiences influenced me to change the first factor of what matters most from People to Passion.

How the One-Page Plan Reinforces What Matters Most

The one-page plan you create using this book works to boost passion, product, productivity, and profits precisely because it embodies simple messages that are meaningful, shows people how they belong to something bigger than themselves, and communicates plainly how they make a difference. Unlike so many other planning models, this one is uncomplicated, unpretentious, and non-threatening. There is no smoke and mirrors behind who prepared it or why. It is intended to be crafted by the very people who work at the company and are most vested in making the decisions that impact their work lives and those of their staffs.

When the plan is completed, it communicates simply to both executives and employees alike at a very direct, visceral level. It is easily grasped and understood. It does not waffle, manipulate or obfuscate the passion behind the company's vision and goals. Its power in synthesizing productivity and profit goals are not lost in 20,000 words and complicated tables and charts.

Anyone can look at this single page—and "get" the company. It is all there in one glance of the eye. It can be pinned on the wall of every employee office, or blown up into a poster for all to see. It is easy to review and update as often as necessary. It can be used to communicate progress to your Board of Directors, who will appreciate its simplicity and clarity.

Most importantly, your one-page plan clearly shows how everything is all linked together. I will explain these linkages in detail throughout the book, but for now, just know that a key benefit is that it vividly demonstrates to employees how their daily jobs are tied to the issues they actually care about—making a difference in the world. They can see how their department's quarterly and annual goals feed into the company's long-term goals, which support its Blue Sky Vision, which is grounded in its Values and based on its Brand Purpose.

I hope that this explanation resonates with you and explains why creating a one-page plan is one of the best things you can do if you are seeking to improve your company's fortunes. I hope you are nodding your head in agreement about how this analysis of human nature can be applied to your company with incredible results.

Let's dive in now and show you how you can create your own one-page plan. Let's start your journey to *Leading With Purpose*. We are excited for you and your company!

CHAPTER SUMMARY

- People crave simple, meaningful messages and want to belong to something bigger than themselves.
- 70% of the US workforce are disengaged—either miserable or apathetic about their jobs—and not reaching their full potential.
- You can help employees see how their short-term goals connect to the company's long-term inspiring story.
- Leaders with passion attract employees with passion.

PREPARING TO CREATE YOUR ONE-PAGE PLAN

To prepare for creating your own one-page plan, we need to review some fundamentals that will help you understand the background to the plan and how you go about constructing it.

Using Our Online Site

This book shows you how to create your company's own one-page plan and then how to use it to engage, empower, and encourage the people you lead. For each section of the plan, we provide you with a detailed description of what goes in it, along with several examples for you to look at. You can use a notebook to fill out your plan as you read this book or gather your team members (explained shortly) and work together on a white board or easel.

In my practice, I initially used a Word document to create the plan for the companies where I was serving as temporary CEO. While this was powerful, it became an enormous administrative challenge to update. I found myself spending my time gathering everyone's updates and summarizing them into the document, then redistributing it. As people became more engaged they made multiple updates on a short-term goal each month. They would send me the information and I would update the plan and send it back out to the entire team. This was a big waste of my precious time. If an executive's time is worth $1000 per hour, you can imagine how costly and inefficient this is.

For this reason, we realized that the entire process had to become automated and exist in the "cloud." So I teamed up with a former Apple technologist, John Bertagnolli, who helped transform my ideas for creating and managing a company from a single page into an online platform. For several years now, our team has enhanced and improved the site based on customer feedback and our own insights into how the plan can be maximized to be effective and valuable to companies. What I am conveying here is that the real power of *Leading With Purpose* is that it coordinates with this online platform our company created, www.LeadWithPurpose.com.

By using our online site to create your plan, you will have access to an easy-to-use tool with many valuable features that will make your work more efficient. Our web site allows you to enter your responses for each element of the plan, update them at any time, and invite an unlimited number of departments to incorporate their annual and quarterly goals into the plan. Any time an authorized user modifies any part of the plan or changes an accountability goal, every team member receives an email indicating the change. Our platform also makes it very easy to print your plan in color on a single sheet of paper. All in all, the Lead With Purpose platform is the most powerful way to use the concepts of this book and share them with your team.

FREE ONLINE TRIAL

You are invited to a free trial to use www.LeadWithPurpose.com to build your plan online. Following the trial period, there is a monthly subscriber fee that is reasonable and beyond competitive with how much it costs you to constantly update a Word document on your own, or bring in a strategic planner or consultant to work with your company each time you feel a need to create a new strategic plan.

Creating Your Plan Involves Both Leadership and Management Thinking

There is an important distinction we make when filling out the elements of your plan—the difference between leadership and management thinking. Large companies, of course, have people whose job is to lead, and other people whose role is to manage employees and processes. In small companies though, the leaders *are* usually the managers; the same people wear both hats. In these circumstances, people often confuse when they should be acting as leaders vs. when they need to think like managers. They often behave like managers when they should be thinking like leaders.

Compounding this situation are people who feel uncomfortable being either a leader or a manager. They often resort to their strength —and either fail to lead when they should lead, or fail to manage when they should manage. Does this describe you by any chance? Or someone in your organization?

One of the most significant advantages of using our process is that it helps you distinguish clearly between leadership and management thinking. If you are responsible for wearing both hats in a small company, it tells you when to wear which hat as you fill out your one-page plan.

What exactly is the difference? To paraphrase one of my favorite quotes about leadership vs. management, Stephen R. Covey said something to this effect: *Management is efficiency in climbing the ladder of success. Leadership is knowing which wall to put the ladder on.* Covey's quote is a great metaphor, but let's expand it a little bit more.

- *Leadership is a visionary capability.* It involves thinking longer term and strategically about the business and its purpose in the world. It is about creating and fostering a culture of like-minded people focused on a shared inspiring view of what the company stands for and where it can go over time. Leadership also involves heart, because it requires passion and a willingness to engage and motivate people. A leader's passion conveys to others how their work is meaningful and creates a better company and world.

- *Management is tactical, immediate, and task-oriented.* It involves thinking shorter term about the operational activities and results of the business. Management sets the annual objectives and quarterly plans to make sure all the manpower and resources are available. Management puts processes and procedures together to make everything operate efficiently to accomplish the long-range plans.

LEADERSHIP
- Long term
- Inspire
- Motivate
- Efficient
- Strategic
- Purpose
- Vision
- Empower
- Culture
- Servant

- Short term
- Objectives
- Logistics
- Efficient
- Manpower
- Organizing
- Daily
- Tactical
- Checklist
- Resources

MANAGEMENT

LONGER

SHORTER

TIMEFRAME

I have spent time thinking about these differences and how they impact planning in both large and small organizations. In large companies, a President usually provides the company with leadership (strategic, long term, inspiring visionary), while a Chief Operating Officer (COO) provides management (short-term planning, daily activities, tactical). When I was in the Navy on a submarine, we had a Captain who provided the leadership and an Executive Officer (XO) who handled the management. When I worked at Honeywell, we had a Branch General Manager for leadership and an Operations Manager for management.

When I began consulting to small organizations, I saw how their lack of resources often prevented them from having separate leadership and management people. Most startups and small companies typically cannot support both a President and a COO position. One person must provide both, shifting quickly between the two mindsets. One day, he or she might lead others to envision where the company will be in ten years, then step outside of the board room and go over to the manufacturing floor to analyze daily production numbers or determine the cause of a machine failure.

The problem in many small companies is that owners believe they are good at only one or the other function. As a result, they fall into doing the one thing they feel most comfortable with. Also, since leaders must show some vulnerability to inspire other people, many shy away from the leadership part. As a result, many small companies miss out on leadership skills that the owner doesn't feel comfortable doing.

One of the powerful aspects of our methodology is that it encourages everyone to become better leaders and managers. It does this by helping you distinguish clearly between your leadership and management functions. No matter what size your company, our approach makes it crystal clear when wearing the leadership or management hat is necessary. In fact, as you go through the seven elements of the plan, you will notice that they are coded for Leadership or Management using the following symbols:

♥ Because leadership is extensively about visioning and inspiring, we symbolize the elements that require leadership using the "heart symbol."

✔ Because management is more task-oriented, we symbolize the elements that involve management with "Check marks."

Laddering the Ideas in Your Plan

I compare creating your one-page plan to building a ladder from the top down. We start at the top rung because, no matter what you want to accomplish in life, you have to identify a goal—where you want to end up. Once you know that, you can work backwards to identify any intermediary mileposts on the way to that goal, and the resources you will need to get there. You can also identify any potential obstacles you might encounter along the way.

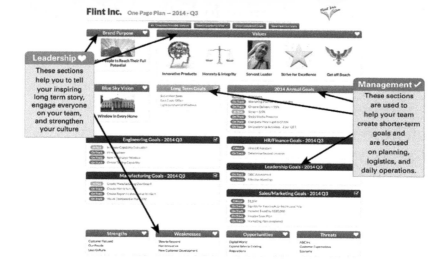

Take the example of a swimmer who has a vision of winning Olympic Gold in the 50 meter freestyle race. She dreams of her winning moment and envisions what it will look and feel like. To get to her goal, she has to build a ladder working backwards to establish the appropriate mileposts along the way. For her, the rungs of the ladder in descending order might be something like the following:

- *Top Rung.* Win Gold at the Olympics within four years.
- *5th Rung.* To win Gold, I need to swim 50 meters faster than the current record of 24.05 seconds.
- *4th Rung.* To swim in the Olympics, I need to be on the US Olympic team.
- *3rd Rung.* To be on the US Olympic team, I need to swim faster than 25.50 seconds at the US qualifiers in three years.
- *2nd Rung.* To make it to the qualifiers, I need to swim 50 meters in 26.75 seconds.
- *1st Rung.* This is where she is today, reflecting on the first 90 days of training of her journey. Here our future Gold winner identifies the immediate tasks she needs, such as hiring a top notch coach.

The five rungs she created above the present day act as her guideposts on the way up, allowing her to measure her progress. As she swims thousands of meters a day and encounters obstacles, she can keep her top-rung vision in front and thus challenge herself to keep getting better. Every 90 days, she evaluates her progress and sets new intermediary goals for the next 90 days. She is always using her inspiring dream of winning Olympic Gold as her top rung.

Creating a strategic plan from the top down is as important for companies as it is for individuals with big goals. This ladder metaphor helps you focus your entire organization on the prize as well as on the milestones to surmount to get there. Holding this image of the business ladder in your mind makes it easier to visualize how we approach filling out a one-page plan because we follow a sequence that mimics constructing a plan from the top down:

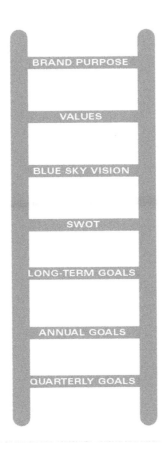

- *Top Rung—Brand Purpose:* The difference you make in the world and the reason your company exists.

- *6th Rung—Values:* The principles you want your company to live by.

- *5th Rung—Blue Sky Vision:* Your 10-year dream of what you want to achieve.

- *4th Rung—SWOT Assessment:* Your strengths, weaknesses, opportunities, and threats.

- *3rd Rung—Long-Term Goals:* Your 5-year realistic goals.

- *2nd Rung—Annual Goals:* Your 1-year goals.

- *1st Rung—Quarterly Goals:* What you want to accomplish in each 90-day period.

This sequence of going through the plan demystifies the strategic planning process. You will find it a pleasure to go through these steps with your team. By the end of the plan, you will be thrilled and impressed at the results your team has achieved. All on a single page, right before your eyes, is the entire game plan for your company to rally behind. It is like putting your dreams and the actions to achieve those dreams onto a single sheet for everyone to witness. This is the magic and the power of creating your own one-page plan.

Assembling a Team

If you want to strengthen your company, get everyone on the same page, and focus your people on what matters most, it makes sense to involve them in preparing your plan. Harvard Business School professor Rosabeth Moss Kanter aptly captured the reason for this when she wrote: "Changes are exciting when done by us—and threatening when done to us."

We recommend that you select a team composed of 5 to 10 people to work on the plan together. More than ten starts to become unmanageable and provides no extra value. Include at least one person from each of the key departments in your company, such as Sales, Marketing, Operations, Human Resources, and Finance. Every company will have a different set of departments, so adjust your list to include those people who are most critical in your company. We will supply specific instructions for how the team will function in the coming sections.

3 Sessions to Create Your Plan

We have found that the ideal way to create your one-page plan is to conduct three sessions with your team in a period of three weeks. In the beginning of the book, we discussed the Engage, Empower, and Encourage approach that any person can learn and use to become a more effective leader. It is no coincidence that the three sessions to complete your one-page plan coincide with the three steps of this approach. More details are below and the chart below summarizes the grouping of the plan elements of each session and our suggested timing.

ONE WEEK IN ADVANCE: PREPARATION FOR SESSION 1
Ask team members to read the sections of the book in which the elements of the session are covered.

Session 1: The Leadership Elements	Total 6 hours
1. Brand Purpose	1 hour
2. Values	1.5 hours
3. Blue Sky Vision (10 Year)	1 hour
4. SWOT	1.5 hours
5. Long-Term (5 Year) Goals	1 hour

ONE WEEK HIATUS: PREPARATION FOR SESSION 2
Ask team members to read the sections of the book in which the elements of the session are covered.

Session 2: The Management Elements	Total 3–4 hours
Note: Between session 1 and 2, the team members responsible for the annual and quarterly goals can review what leadership has determined to be the Brand Purpose, Values, Blue Sky Vision, SWOT, and Long-Term goals. This will help them think ahead about their annual and quarterly goals before they attend Session 2.	
1. Annual Goals	1 hour
2. Current Quarterly Goals	2–3 hours
Hours depend on how many teams are developing quarterly goals.	

ONE WEEK HIATUS: PREPARATION FOR SESSION 3
Ask team members to read the sections of the book in which the elements of the session are covered.

Session 3: Reviewing Your Plan & Assigning Symbols	Total 3 hours
1. Review the entire plan and make adjustments	1 hour
2. Find and assign symbols and icons to the various elements of the plan	2 hours

- *Session 1: Leadership. (6 hours)* This is devoted to the elements of the plan that require leadership thinking. Given the three truths I discovered about human nature, it is the team's job to identify the company's meaningful story—its higher purpose, vision, and values for people to connect with and feel part of. You will use what you create here to Engage employees and customers.

- *Session 2: Management. (3 to 4 hours)* This focuses your team on the elements that require management thinking. When this session is complete, each employee will see what their top three goals are today and how these connect all the way up to the story crafted in Session 1. Now you will have everything you need to start Empowering employees and push decision making down to them.

• *Session 3: Finalize Plan. (3 hours)* This involves reviewing your plan, making any edits to the final wording, and choosing symbols (explained shortly). The content from this session is used to create simple recognition programs for Encouraging employees as they implement and bring the plan to life.

All in all, most teams can get through all of this in about 12 or 13 hours. We do recommend that you allow at least one week in between each session. Chunking it up into three small bite-sized sessions is less stressful and will help the team produce a better plan. Here is why.

First, breaking up the sessions allows team members to focus more deeply on just a few components at a time and they will feel less stressed by not being gone multiple days in a row.

Second, the time in between the sessions is valuable. Team members can work with other employees to get their feedback and involvement in creating goals. The time also allows people to reflect on the ideas from the previous session. Often, teams find the essence of the Brand Purpose or the Blue Sky Vision, but not the exact wording. The time in between helps the ideas from the previous meeting to percolate. I have often seen someone show up in the next session with the exact wording that resonates with the entire team.

Once you have picked your team, have a kick-off meeting that is no longer than 30 minutes. Describe the entire process with dates for each of the sessions. During this time we recommend you provide each member a copy of this book and the results of any customer or employee survey feedback you have.

Session 1 should be conducted live and in-person, even if it means bringing in team members who work remotely. While virtual meetings are acceptable, having the team together for the first round boosts the energy and involvement of individuals. It also allows the CEO, President, or leader to establish the rules for creating the plan while inspiring team members to recognize the importance and value of it.

After you meet in person for this first Session, it is fine to do Sessions 2 and 3 using online meeting tools such as Skype or Goto Meeting. We understand that it is difficult to arrange a time compatible with everyone's busy schedule, and since Sessions 2 and 3 are shorter, it may not make sense to bring in people from a distance for these.

Strive for Simplicity

I was led to develop a one-page plan when I learned to Keep it Simple, Short, and Clear. We need you and your team to do the same. We have provided you a unique format that has a distinguishing characteristic: everything that matters to your company will be synthesized on a single sheet. Gone are pages and pages of writing that complicate the simple statements that everyone can understand and assimilate into their hearts and minds.

Don't think of the plan you create as an abbreviated version of a longer 10 or 30 page strategic document that other strategy consultants believe you should have. No matter how beautifully written, designed and published they are, traditional strategic plans get put on shelves and are seldom looked at again. You will see that a one-page plan, in its honest simplicity, is the only document you need to get people focused on what matters most and drive your company to success.

"The ability to simplify means to eliminate the unnecessary so that the necessary may speak." — HANS HOFFMANN, Famous Abstract Painter

Consult Employee and Customer Surveys

Having employee and customer surveys on hand to guide your team in completing sections of your plan can prove useful. Surveys often illuminate what your employees or customers think about your company. They can often reveal truths you may not have understood before, or they can add just the right insight to make your ideas come alive. If you have recently conducted employee or customer surveys, consult those results unless they are more than a year old. If so, send out new surveys to update your data.

We have created a guide to doing employee and customer surveys that you can obtain in our resources section online. The guide provides step-by-step instructions on everything you need to perform and analyze a customer or employee survey. It includes sample questions in English and Spanish and emails to customers and employees to help you maximize participation. I have found that you get far better feedback when you assure participants that their answers are anonymous; no one will know who made what comment. Employees are also more willing to take a survey if they know the total results will be presented back to them.

It is quite easy today to generate, distribute, collect, and analyze customer surveys using an online survey tool. For instance, Survey Monkey provides users with basic functionality for free, and more features for a small monthly fee. If any of your workers do not have email or an online access tool is not available, you can create your own survey document in all the languages you need, print them out, and ask employees to fill it out manually. If you plan on performing new surveys, please allot two additional weeks before your kickoff meeting to complete the surveys and summarize the results. Once the analysis summaries have been completed, dispense them to the entire team in advance of the first session for their review and use in creating your plan.

How to Translate an Existing Plan

You might have an existing strategic plan with valuable content to maintain. The problem is, your plan may use different terminology than that proposed in this book. If so, here is a "table of correspondences" that lists each of the components of the one-page plan you will build and various common terms that other planning models often use.

OUR TERMINOLOGY	SIMILAR TERMINOLOGY
Brand Purpose	Purpose, Mission, Brand Promise, Value proposition, Reason you exist, Difference you make in the world
	Note: The terms Target Market, Primary Market, and Primary Customers fit into your Brand Purpose. If you use our online platform, you can enter this sub-set of information in a subsection of Brand Purpose.
Values	Core Values, Beliefs
Blue Sky Vision	Vision, BHAG, Moonshot
SWOT • Strengths • Weaknesses • Opportunities • Threats	Internal/External Analysis
	Strengths—Competitive Advantages, Capabilities, Unique Assets, Core Competency, Strategic Advantage inside your company.
	Weaknesses—Disadvantages, Lack of Resources, or Vulnerabilities you have inside your company.
	Opportunities (positive) and **Threats** (negative)—Center around how external political, legislative, technological, economic, and competitive factors and trends may affect you.
Long Term Goals	Strategies, Mileposts, Initiatives, Priorities, Objectives
Annual Goals	One Year Goals
Quarterly Goals	90 Day Goals

How to Proceed Through This Book

If you are the CEO or President, we suggest that you read on and become familiar with all remaining chapters on your own first. Feel free to write down your own answers to each component of the plan. It is prudent for you to have thought through the Brand Purpose, Values, Blue Sky Vision, and long-term goals as your team may look to you for direction when you begin to work with them to create the answers.

However, we also believe it is invaluable to ask your entire team to read through the book and come with their own set of ideas. Reading it themselves better prepares them for the work you will perform as a team.

A small investment in extra copies of the book will go a long way to obtaining exceptional results because you will enable everyone on your team to be on the same page with you. This way, when you start building your plan, everyone has already devoted time and thought to each component and your meetings will be more effective and efficient.

CHAPTER SUMMARY

- Companies need a balance of both Leadership (longer-term inspiring story) and Management (short-term goals) thinking.
- Use the ladder concept to understand how the Leadership and Management elements are tightly connected.
- The best way to use this book is to complete three sessions one week apart.
- Adopt the Engage, Empower, and Encourage leadership approach to help your people achieve their full potential.

SESSION 1

COMPLETING THE LEADERSHIP ELEMENTS

ONE

Finding Your
Brand Purpose

I wrote that one of the strongest needs of human nature is to relate to a meaningful message or story that expresses how we are all connected to a higher purpose. A powerful purpose message is what companies use to keep employees engaged and attract the best employees who share the company's passion. It also attracts customers who love your brand and want to do business with your company. For this reason, the first component of your one-page plan is creating a powerful statement that reflects your *Brand Purpose*.

What is a Brand Purpose?

You may not have heard the term "Brand Purpose" before. It merges two concepts that are vital to any company's survival. One of these is "purpose," which some strategy planning refers to as your "mission." In traditional planning, a company's mission statement was largely an internally-focused phrasing intended for employees. It informed them of how the company viewed its reason for existence and stated the value it contributed in the marketplace. This helped employees understand their ultimate goal.

The second component of "Brand Purpose" relates to branding—the increasingly important science of making your company distinctive in the eyes of your customer. Many strategists talk about having a clear "brand promise" statement so that customers know what they can expect from you, whether it be the most innovative technology, the highest quality products, the best in service excellence, or the most entertaining experience.

Traditionally, employees and customers have different perspectives of a company. For the employees, they have a responsibility to achieve profitability, but the best employees also want to know they are making a difference in the world. From the customer's perspective, they are primarily looking to have a need fulfilled, but they, too, want to know they can depend on the company to provide a meaning they can identify with.

In our view, the most powerful message a company can have speaks to both employees and customers. This is why the two concepts were combined into "Brand Purpose." This term amalgamates the most meaningful aspects of your company's mission and combines it with your brand promise to customers to create a vibrant and emotionally powerful statement that inspires everyone, internally and externally.

An inspiring Brand Purpose drives the best people to want to work with you and stay at your company. A clear Brand Purpose helps employees manage the ambiguity of the day-to-day challenges they face. No obstacle is too large and no challenge is too great to overcome. They are engaged and passionate about their work, willing to go the extra mile, exerting themselves beyond their job definitions to perform extra-role behaviors. Your Brand Purpose is also an exciting message that appeals to your customers and turns them into loyal brand fans who believe in your products or services and are eager to tell everyone else about them.

How does a great Brand Purpose achieve these results? Recall a time when you felt passionate about something and clearly understood the reason you wanted to do it. Perhaps it was when you were young and played a sport, or when you were in college studying French or chemistry. Or maybe it was when you created a new product and started your business. The purpose of why you were doing what you were doing was very clear and you were inspired. You easily lost track of time practicing your skills or studying for a test or getting your product to market. Nothing stood in your way; it didn't feel like "work," and setbacks were mere obstacles to overcome. People who came into contact with you were "infected" with inspiration. In short, you were *emotionally connected and engaged*.

This is the impact a powerful Brand Purpose has on employees and customers. It charges them emotionally, and they feel engaged with your company. They become committed to you and willing to do whatever it takes to support the company. They share your passion because your message helps them feel they are taking part in something meaningful and making a contribution to the world.

Let's look at a few strong examples of Brand Purpose.

• Google's purpose is, "We organize the world's information and make it universally accessible and useful." This single statement is not only a big promise to customers that they can use Google to search for the "world's information;" it also acts as a mantra for leadership and employees reminding them that their daily actions are making a difference in the world. The words "world" and "universally" imply that Google is reaching to impact everyone on this planet.

• Nike's purpose is: "To bring Inspiration and Innovation to Every Athlete* in the World."(*If you have a body, you are an athlete).

This statement speaks to both employees and customers on an emotional level. Employees are excited knowing that they can be an inspiration to every other human being on the planet by creating innovative athletic footwear and accessories. Customers are inspired knowing that at least one person or company, namely Nike, believes in them and that they possess athletic ability.

How to Formulate Your Brand Purpose

A great Brand Purpose is an enduring statement of meaning. Some say the statement needs to continue being relevant for at least 50 years into the future to be enduring. It is usually composed of a single terse statement, using between just five and ten words.

In a Harvard Business Review article, *Determining Your Company's Vision*, Jim Collins and Jerry Porras offer some additional ideas to consider when you are fashioning your purpose.[3] They write that a good purpose has to have at least the following characteristics:

1. It is inspiring and helps to stimulate change.
2. It can never be reached.
3. It reflects people's idealistic motivations for doing the company's work.

How do you go about figuring out the phrasing of your Brand Purpose? A good method to follow is to begin by asking yourself and your team questions like the following:

- What difference do we make in the world?
- Why does our company exist?
- What role do we play in the marketplace and society?
- What promise are we fulfilling for our customers?
- What inspires our employees to be proud of where they work?

If you are struggling to answer these questions with surety, tap into your employees and customers to see how they view your company. If you have current employee and customer surveys, then review these for insights. If you would like help completing a new survey, go to www.LeadWithPurpose.com to see sample questionnaires and directions. You will want to look at the responses to these specific questions:

From Employee Survey Questions

- Why do you think this company exists?
- Why do you like working here?
- What has been your proudest moment while working here?

- What three words come to mind when you hear our company name?
- Why do you buy from us?
- What pain point or specific problem do we solve for you?

Another way to find the best phraseology is to put your products on a table or place photos of them at the top of an easel pad or a whiteboard, then ask the question "Why does that matter?" Go around the room and have each team member answer the question about why your product(s) make a difference in the world.

As you develop some first wording, keep in mind that the best Brand Purposes have an emotional component. It cannot be a rather flat, uninspiring commonality like "We make the best products."

Companies that take time to develop a compelling, inspiring, and memorable Brand Purpose statement will win the most important asset—the hearts of their employees and customers. This step can be a very exciting process that also helps inspire your team to go through the rest of the sessions with passion.

Remember: Every human being wants to belong to something bigger than themselves and delights in knowing how they might be changing people's lives in some way. Your company's Brand Purpose should respond to the need for a powerful story or message if you are going to inspire potential and current employees and customers. Make sure that employees can easily see how what they are doing today contributes to your company's Brand Purpose. People go above and beyond when they understand this link.

As you wordsmith your Brand Purpose, allow time for people's ideas to percolate. You may not find the perfect wording right away. Don't worry. You have several chances to come back to revise it later.

Case Study

The YWCA of San Diego County helps women, children, and families escape domestic violence and homelessness, overcome trauma, rebuild their lives, and achieve self-sufficiency. They run five facilities and provide comprehensive services that include safe housing, counseling, legal assistance, employment support, financial literacy training, and supportive children's programs. They serve over 5,000 individuals annually in San Diego County.

The YWCA used a Lead With Purpose coach to help them create their own one-page plan. To formulate its Brand Purpose, the team listed all of the programs that it provides at the top of a whiteboard. It also gathered and reviewed customer and employee feedback about the YWCA that it had received throughout the years.

Customer comments centered around positive statements like: "You saved my life," "Thank you for giving me a safe place to stay," "Thank you for helping me navigate the legal system and obtain a restraining order," and "The employment services program helped me find a job so I can support myself and my two children."

Employee comments included statements like: "I like helping a woman to understand her true potential," "I like seeing how my program positively impacts people," and "I like advocating for women and families."

The team then put their programs at the top of the whiteboard and started asking "Why Does that Matter?" They continued asking this question for each answer they developed in a series of "And why does that matter" questions.

Why does the YWCA of San Diego County Matter?

We provide programs and services and a safe environment for survivors of domestic violence and homeless women, children, and families.

And why does that matter?

The safe environment allows people to fully focus on, and finish, the programs we provide. They are no longer worrying about the next incidence of violence or being homeless, and they can focus on learning new skills and all the tools available to them to rebuild their lives.

The women and children who finish the programs we offer have a much higher success rate of breaking the cycle of domestic violence and homelessness.

By breaking the cycle of domestic violence and homelessness, we are helping people to positively transform themselves and their lives.

This last statement resonated with the team. They could imagine that when a woman is asked what the YWCA provides her, instead of saying "I attended their counseling and employment support programs," she could say *"They helped me transform my life."* The team also looked at this statement from the employee's perspective. Instead of an employee saying "I run a counseling program at the YWCA," he or she could be inspired to say, *"I help transform people's lives."*

After some additional refining, the Brand Purpose of the YWCA of San Diego County became *"Transforming Lives Together."*

The team then tested their new statement by asking four questions.

Is it succinct? YES
Is it inspiring to employees? YES
Is it inspiring to customers? YES
Will it be relevant 50 years from now? YES

Even after we are long gone, the statement should inspire other employees, clients, and donors in 50 years.

***

The Brand Purpose exercise proved very fruitful for this organization. As Heather Finlay, CEO of the YWCA of San Diego County, shared with me, "We provide a variety of programs and wrap-around support services. Finding a succinct and memorable statement that is relevant to our employees and the community was eye opening and a lot of fun for our team. "Transforming Lives

Together" not only resonated with our employees, it has been well received by our donors. This process was a great start for us, and we will continue to engage our employees, customers, and donors to refine our messaging, our long-term goals, and the best ways to transform lives together."

CHAPTER SUMMARY

What is a Brand Purpose?

It is the reason your company exists and the difference your products or services are making in the world. It is also the promise your company delivers relative to your customer expectations. It is sometimes referred to as your mission, and is a simple and memorable statement that can have relevance for more than 50 years.

Why is a Brand Purpose Important?

People fall in love with the company they work at if they feel their work is relevant and they can easily understand how their daily activities are linked to a higher purpose. Driven by a feeling of purpose beyond earning a paycheck, the employee's passion will inspire them to go the extra mile. A great Brand Purpose boosts employee engagement and customer loyalty.

My ideas for how to express our Brand Purpose:

TWO

Determining Your
Company Values

Whenever people work or interact with each other, a culture is created. But what guides this culture? What determines if it is a benevolent, happy, open, and courteous culture—or a cut-throat, secretive, rumor-mongering, overworked, cut-corners culture?

The answer is—values. At the core of any culture, there must be a set of values. This is as true for businesses as it is for society. It doesn't matter if your business employs two people or 20,000, values need to exist. Those values can be determined by the leaders of the culture, or they can be determined collaboratively by all participants in the culture. Organizations with strong values live more harmoniously, manage change better, last longer, and are more prosperous.

Unless someone consciously decides on what those values are, the culture will fall automatically into the values that the most assertive people have. This can be disastrous in organizations that fail to control their values. This situation often leads to cultures where unethical behaviors, fraud, lax standards, disregard for customers, and disrespect for employees take over.

Enron is perhaps one of the most famous examples of a culture that allowed, even encouraged, fraud to run rampant throughout the top ranks of its top executives. This culture led to the one of the worst instances of corporate fraud in the US. Billions of dollars of debt were hidden through financial loopholes, resulting in the company's sudden bankruptcy and the loss of thousands of jobs and billions of dollars in shareholder investment.

The importance of determining your company's values cannot be underestimated. That is why they follow in importance immediately behind Brand Purpose.

What are Values?

Values are defined as deeply-held beliefs and principles that guide every instance of decision making among the leaders of your company. Your values stand behind how employees treat each other and how everyone in your company interacts with customers. Your values must be rock solid and permanent. They cannot be sacrificed even for short term benefits nor can they be applied subjectively to different situations. They are the fabric of your company and, as such, they last forever.

In our experience, a company typically benefits from defining no more than five values. The terms you choose might reflect various aspects about your business, such as what you believe about:

- the rules of doing business
- the way you want to treat employees
- the promises you make to satisfy your customers
- the way you will approach the future
- the importance you give to learning
- the commitment you make to social causes

The cereal company Kellogg's uses the following statement to express their values: "Through integrity, accountability, passion, humility, simplicity and a focus on success, we have created a vibrant company culture where ideas can blossom, people can thrive and success can flourish." The words in boldface are actually their list of six values, and the rest of the statement shows how the company believes their values drive their success.

Another example of a strong set of values comes from Rackspace, a global leader in cloud computing. In 2014, it was ranked by *Fortune* magazine #29 on the annual list of 100 Best Companies to Work For. The culture is so strong that employees there are referred to as Rackers. Before potential employees submit an application, they are asked whether the values listed on the website "ring true and whether they could hold themselves and each other accountable for living these values on a daily basis." The values they list are:

1. Fanatical Support® in all we do
2. Results first, substance over flash
3. Committed to Greatness
4. Full Disclosure and Transparency
5. Passion for our Work
6. Treat fellow Rackers like Friends and Family

These are just two examples of famous companies and their unique set of values for their specific culture. In the resource section online at www.LeadWithPurpose.com, we have listed the top 50 values for you to look at.

How to Determine Your Values?

Creating your values requires the input of your company's top leaders and ideally your employees, but senior leadership must be the final arbiters because the values need to support your Brand Purpose.

Begin by looking at the values that already exist in your organization. Even if you've never developed a formal set of values, the fact is, they are already there. It is your job to discover them, then decide if these are the values to keep. Think of the process as learning about what values people now live by, examining and refining them, and then announcing and promoting the new set of values, making sure that everyone recognizes the changes you are making.

Next, look at the values your company founder may have established, even if that person is no longer alive or active in the company. Try to assess what values he or she imposed on the company culture, explicitly or implicitly. If you are the founder of the company, ask yourself what values you have consciously or unconsciously embedded into the culture.

Next, review any employee and customer surveys (or if you have time, send out a new one) to ascertain if the responses help you fathom what values people already think your company has. If you are sending out anew, ask your employees why they like working at your company and what they believe to be your strengths.

Finally, review your company's most important successes for hints about what they tell you about your values. For instance, what are the attributes of your best employees? Can you use those to model values that you want other employees to have? What do customers say about your company's greatest achievements? Can those reactions become elements of your values?

Brainstorm with your team and write down all of the values on an easel or board where everyone can see them. Then seek to combine similar terms together. One employee might have said Honesty as a value. Later in the list you see the word Integrity and further down the word Trust. You could combine these three into one group and choose the group heading to be Honesty.

Finally, take a vote to prioritize the top five values that you want to reflect your company. Write them down and see how they feel to you and your team. Do not discard the other words that were in each group. As an example, Honesty is the value and the words Trust and Integrity are two words that can be used to describe the Honesty value in depth. All of the words associated with your top five values can be used to start your own company vocabulary.

CHAPTER SUMMARY

What are Values?

Values are the principles that guide decision making and how employees interact with each other and with your customers. They can't be sacrificed or applied subjectively to different situations. They are the DNA of your company and last forever.

Why are Values Important?

Whenever people work or interact with each other, a culture is created. As it was with the earliest civilizations, it is the same today for businesses. At the core of a strong culture are well-defined values that are extremely obvious through the use of symbols, behaviors, and rituals. Strong cultures live more harmoniously, manage change better, last longer, and are more prosperous.

NOTES

My ideas for what our company's values are:

THREE

Creating a Blue Sky Vision

Close your eyes and envision where your company will be in ten years. Don't just think of where it is going, actually *DREAM* about where it could be if all your wishes were to come true. Imagine that time in the future when there are no storms on the horizon—nothing but clear skies as you sail forward.

This is your Blue Sky Vision (BSV)—a future image of your company that assumes the best of results for you. All your barriers have been toppled; all your challenges have been overcome. As a company, you are making an impact on the world. You have the best employees who are happy about coming to work, you are financially stable, and you have a loyal customer following.

Why Have a Blue Sky Vision?

Having a BSV is invaluable because it encourages you to look into the future and see how you want to grow and shape your company. It stretches your mind to the possibilities of what you can accomplish over an extended period of time. It acts as a focal point for the entire organization in terms of what you will strive to do and who you can become in the world.

Your BSV links up directly to your Brand Purpose in that it envisions how the company will evolve and live out its purpose for employees and customers. In effect, it targets challenging and positive long-range goals that you commit to seek in line with your Brand Purpose.

One of the most famous Blue Sky Visions is President John F. Kennedy's 1961 statement that America would commit to landing a man on the moon and return him safely to earth "before this decade is out." Kennedy's vision of space exploration provoked an amazingly productive decade of scientific and technological innovation, ranging from rockets to space suits to freeze dried food and Tang. His vision was so powerful that it inspired ongoing innovation even after his death in 1963. Ever since Kennedy's vision of a moon landing within a decade, many have thought of Blue Sky Visioning as a 10-year exercise. Some people even refer to it as "creating a moon shot."

How to Formulate a Blue Sky Vision

How does one go about creating a BSV? Does it mean inventing a fantasy, intentionally making it unreasonable and unattainable to push yourselves to the edge? Do you exaggerate your imagination to the nth degree or to a point of totally zaniness and call it a Blue Sky Vision?

No, this doesn't work. To create a meaningful BSV, begin by listing real accomplishments you want to achieve ten years from now. These should be grounded in the history of your company—things that you have already achieved and know you can do in a certain timeframe—while at the same time projecting your capabilities into the future under the most positive of circumstances. In your ideal world scenario, you are able to overcome most barriers to your business. You can get the technology you need. You have the right people and enough resources. Given this freedom, ask yourself questions like the following about the period ten years from today:

1. What products and services do we provide?
2. Who are our customers?
3. How many employees do we have?
4. How many offices do we have?
5. What do the facilities and offices look like?
6. What are our annual revenues?
7. What significant goals have we accomplished?
8. What awards and recognition have we earned?

9. How do we impact the world?

10. What problems do our customers look to us to solve?

If you can answer these types of questions, you are on your way to formulating a BSV. Work with your team to collate and refine the visions everyone offers. Your goal is now to create a headline that best represents your Blue Sky Vision. It is similar to the headline of a newspaper article. In your team session, make a list of up to five versions of the BSV on a whiteboard or easel, then use the process of elimination to remove those that are less promising or interesting than others, or combine several versions into a single statement. Work upwards towards the most interesting and challenging BSV, rather than choosing the easiest one. In short, stretch yourselves and aim for achieving the highest vision possible, not the easiest.

Setting a stimulating and exciting BSV has many benefits, especially for employees. If you have the right BSV, it can become a story that allows you to attract people who believe in that same vision. A great BSV inspires people to want to work at your company and remain there, just to be part of the team that reaches the pinnacle of success you define for your future.

Here is a good example of a Blue Sky Vision from one of the most imaginative companies in the world, Amazon. In 2007, Amazon released its first Kindle e-book reader into the world. In his letter to shareholders, Amazon's CEO Jeff Bezos wrote, "Our vision for Kindle is every book ever printed in any language, all available in less than 60 seconds." Back in 2007, whoever would have thought this was doable? It seemed farfetched, but it was a "moonshot" that Amazon believed it could reach.

Today, not even a decade later, Amazon is close to achieving this BSV. The Kindle has been improved through six generations of technological enhancements, going from its first generation machine up to the newest Kindle Fire HD machines that run on Android platforms and are more like tablet computers. Kindle software is available for computers and even for competitor iPad devices, so no matter what device you are using, you can read a Kindle e-book. While no one can say exactly how many Kindle devices have been sold, we know that Kindles have changed the world of publishing. More e-books have been sold in recent years than hardcover books. Jeff Bezos dreamed a Blue Sky Vision and brought it to fruition as much as John F. Kennedy's promise took America to the moon and back.

CHAPTER SUMMARY

What is a Blue Sky Vision?

It is a 10-year goal that aligns under your company's Brand Purpose. It is not easily achievable and will stretch your company and its resources. A well-conceived Blue Sky Vision will also inspire and excite both customers and employees.

Why is a Blue Sky Vision Important?

Setting the proper Blue Sky Vision can have many benefits; the most important one is for employees. If you have the right employees who are inspired by and understand what the Blue Sky Vision is, you will see them focus all of their efforts and go to extraordinary lengths to achieve it.

NOTES

My ideas for our company's BSV include:

FOUR

Assessing Your
Strengths, Weaknesses,
Opportunities & Threats

You are probably familiar with this well-known management exercise known as a SWOT Analysis, the acronym for assessing your Strengths, Weaknesses, Opportunities, and Threats. Performing a SWOT analysis is not a quick and dirty reflection on these four areas, but rather a highly structured exercise that is done with care and attention.

A SWOT looks internally at your company's strengths and weaknesses, and externally at your company's opportunities and threats. The results of a well-done SWOT analysis will help your organization assess what it needs to do to achieve the Brand Purpose and Blue Sky Vision you created for your company, as well as to reassess any elements that need correction or refinement.

How to Perform a SWOT Analysis

Having your team of people together for the SWOT analysis is valuable, as each person brings in perspectives from their experience that others don't have. The best approach is to take each section of the SWOT and discuss it separately. Each section has its own set of questions that will help you elicit and analyze the thinking you need to move forward.

Strengths Questions

A strength is any internal talent, skill, competency, technology, individual, or relationship that brings the company competitive advantage. It can include high quality manufacturing processes, a talented sales team, a strategic relationship with a supplier, a superior product, or another quality that gives you an edge over competitors. Answer these questions from your own perspective as well as from what you know about the perspectives of your customers and employees:

1. Why do customers choose to buy from you?
2. What do employees see as your strengths that make them want to work there?
3. What is unique about your service or product?
4. What strategic relationships do only you have?

Once you have answered these questions, discuss what resources you need and what activities you need to keep doing to maintain your strength position.

Weaknesses Questions

A weakness is the opposite of a strength—talent, resources, competencies, relationships, individuals, processes, technologies and so on—that you lack internally and does not support your competitive advantage. It might be your outdated manufacturing equipment, an old CRM system, or an aging workforce. From your own perspective, as well as from that of your employees and customers, answer these questions:

1. What prevents customers from buying from you?
2. What have your customers told you needs to get better?
3. Why do customers complain?
4. What do your employees see as the company's weakness?

Once you have answered these questions, discuss the following:

• What resources do you need and what actions might you take to remove each weakness from this list?
• What do you need to do to counter a weakness that your competitors and customers are aware of?

Opportunities Questions

Assessing your opportunities is largely an external facing exercise. You want to analyze what conditions in the outside world might allow you to exploit your strengths or make up for your weaknesses. For instance, an opportunity might be a new market opening up due to advances in technology, a new customer appearing, a cheaper supplier, the ability to outsource manufacturing, or a major competitor going out of business. Take a look at your internal strengths and see where you can take advantage of external conditions. Answer these questions:

1. Any societal or cultural changes you are aware of?
2. Any opportunity to take what you sell to other markets?
3. Any shifts in technology?
4. Any negative changes for your competitors?

Once you have answered these, discuss if any of your internal strengths can help you take advantage of the opportunities identified.

Threat Questions

A threat is an external change in economic conditions, markets, competition, or social trends that worsens your position. It might be the appearance of new technology that makes yours obsolete or a price reduction by a competitor, or a new barrier that prevents you from expanding a market of yours, or a change in tax rates or medical costs that will detract from your cash flow. Answer these questions:

1. Any changes to policy that affect your business?
2. Any new competitors in your market?
3. Any positive market positions for your competitors?
4. Any changes to technology?

Once you have answered these questions, discuss the following:

• What do you need to do and what resources do you need to reduce a threat?
• Do you have any strengths that could help you reduce a threat?

Case Study

Here's an example from a small manufacturing firm. The team used customer and employee survey results and customer feedback from the last year to produce their own SWOT.

STRENGTHS	WEAKNESSES
• Why do customers choose to buy from you? • What do your employees see as your strengths? • What is unique about your service or product?	• What prevents customers from buying from you? • Are there internal areas that need improvement? • Which factors cause customer complaints?
• Our innovative people • Concept and deliver • Manufacturing capabilities • Reputation in the industry • Provider of custom solutions	• Internal communications • Lead times • Inventory process — transactions • Manufacturing errors • Sales concentrated in few customers
OPPORTUNITIES	THREATS
• Can you take what you sell to other markets? • Any shifts in technology? • Any changes in competitive landscape?	• Any changes to policy that affect your business? • Any new competitors in your market? • What are competitors doing that worries you?
• New production • Increase existing market share • Increasing offshore manufacturing costs	•Worldwide economic slowdown • Healthcare • Migration to new technologies

This SWOT analysis helped the company create action plans and budget for resources that allowed them to strengthen their strategy going forward in the future. Overall, it made both leadership and management more aware of their challenges and better able to react and plan. The company decided, for example, that it would put a high priority on reducing their errors so they would have fewer rejected products. This would increase their reputation among customers for being a leader in precision products. Secondly, given that they were respected for being innovators, they built special teams of sales and engineering specialists who worked directly with customers to solve their problems.

The company also began developing many new products in joint ventures with their customers, which helped solidify their relationships and made it harder for competitors to win over existing customers based solely on price. Regarding opportunities, they used their innovation capability to enter some new markets, including medical devices and home appliances. Knowing that some competitors were doing well with wireless devices, the firm opted to purchase a small competitor who held the patent on some wireless technologies, thus providing them with capabilities in both wired and wireless markets.

As this case study shows, a SWOT analysis is invaluable to a company in many ways. If you have not done one yet, we are confident you will find performing a formal SWOT analysis to be highly illuminating and insightful.

CHAPTER SUMMARY

What is a SWOT Analysis?

A SWOT is a powerful tool for you and your team to uncover and understand what your Strengths and Weaknesses are. It also helps you to identify Opportunities you should take advantage of and Threats you need to be aware of. Strengths and Weaknesses are internal to your company while Opportunities and Threats are external.

Why is a SWOT Analysis Important?

A well-formulated SWOT will help you to focus and assign resources to strengthen your position or protect you from any threats. The barrier to entry into any business segment is lower than ever so it is important to keep an eye on the competition.

NOTES

My ideas for our company's SWOT analysis include:

STRENGTHS	WEAKNESSES
• Why do customers choose to buy from you? • What do your employees see as your strengths? • What is unique about your service or product?	• What prevents customers from buying from you? • Are there internal areas that need improvement? • Which factors cause customer complaints?
OPPORTUNITIES	**THREATS**
• Can you take what you sell to other markets? • Any shifts in technology? • Any changes in competitive landscape?	• Any changes to policy that affect your business? • Any new competitors in your market? • What are competitors doing that worries you?

FIVE

Setting Long-Term Goals

It is important to have a set of long-term goals focused on the not-so-distant future. Your long-term goals can be targeted at financial, operational, or people-related matters. While there are other areas to focus on, most for-profit companies focus on growth of revenues, number of products offered, or size of customer base while non-profits focus may be in the areas of number of people served, total $ raised, or number of donors.

Long-term goals are based on provable facts and numbers, or educated guesses grounded in reality. While your Blue Sky Vision imagines your company in the most positive, ideal context, your long-term goals take into account the realities of market barriers, competition, resources, and performance history. They are down-to-earth, reasonable projections of what you believe you can achieve.

It should be noted that the creation of long-term goals is a management function, but is intentionally completed in Session 1. The week in between the sessions gives team members the opportunity to bring the three long-term goals to their employees and then work together with them to create their annual and quarterly goals which are then presented in Session 2.

How to Formulate Long-Term Goals

We recommend that long-term goals use five years as the best timeframe to look ahead. In some industries, it is better to use three years if the pace of change is too great and predicting new technologies, competitors, or market forces five years down the road is impractical if not impossible.

I compare the process of creating long-term goals to wearing bifocals. It requires both Leadership and Management thinking. You need to have some degree of leadership vision to look into the future because your long-term goals need to support achieving your Blue Sky Vision and ultimately lead you towards your Brand Purpose. At the same time, however, you also need to consider the present time to ground your long-term goals in predictions that are actionable, reasonable, and affordable. In fact, in the next section, you will be preparing annual and quarterly goals aligned with your long-term goals. This means that your long-term goals must be translatable into more immediate goals that impact people this year and this quarter. In this sense, developing long-term goals is both strategic and tactical.

How many long-term goals should you set? We recommend no more than three to five for the company as a whole. You don't want your team members wasting time creating a long list of detailed goals that are unrealistic, bordering on hypothetical. It is far better to focus on three really achievable long-term goals that people can have confidence in trying to achieve.

For example, if you are small business, you might have five-year long-term goals of tripling your customers, expanding service to all the Western states, and adding three new products. This might be reasonable if your industry is highly competitive and you know that it takes years to incrementally build your customer base, grow revenues, and develop marketable new products. And if such long-term goals supported your Blue Sky Vision of becoming the #1 company in your industry within 10 years, you'd know they are appropriate and useful.

The SMART Method of Checking Your Long-Term Goals

There is a technique we recommend using to ensure your long-term goals are clearly stated, useful, and meaningful. Called the SMART method, it stands for identifying goals that are Specific, Measurable, Achievable, Relevant, and Time frame appropriate. Here is a chart showing how a runner might identify goals and how they can be improved by applying the SMART method to rephrase them.

	ORIGINAL	HOW TO IMPROVE	IMPROVED STATEMENT
Specific	"I want to move faster."	Not specific. Do you mean run faster or walk faster? Faster than other people or a dog? Be specific about your goal and make it clear what it is. Remove ambiguities.	"Finish in top ten of my age group in the Vista 10k race" is specific.
Measurable	"I want to run faster."	Vague and not measurable. Your goal must be easy to track progress on and you need to be able to identify when you hit your goal.	"I want to reduce my mile time from 9 min. to 7 min." is measurable.
Achievable	"Reduce my mile time from 9 min. to 7 min. by the end of this week."	Probably unrealistic. Don't set yourself up for failure by being too aggressive. With an achievable goal you can determine needed resources.	"Reduce my mile time from 9 min. to 7 min. in three months" is achievable with effort and training.
Relevant	"I want cut my lawn in less than 45 minutes."	Not relevant to running goal. Your goals need to be relevant to your business and make an impact when reached.	"I will train four times a week" is a relevant goal to winning the Vista 10K race.
Time Frame	"I will win my age group of the Vista 10k race."	No time frame. Having a clear end date gives you a finish line to shoot for and creates a sense of urgency.	"In three years, I will win my age group at the Vista 10k race" contains a clear time frame.

Be Sure to Align Your Long-Term Goals

It is also important to check your long-term goals to ensure they align with your Brand Purpose, Values, Blue Sky Vision, and your SWOT analysis. Are you neglecting a goal you would need to achieve your Blue Sky Vision in ten years? Is any long-term goal contradictory to your Brand Purpose? Would a profit goal you want to achieve cause you to abandon any of your values? Are the goals supported by what you have identified as your strengths and opportunities? Did you fail to take into account any weaknesses or threats that need to be tackled before you can achieve those long-term goals? This alignment proofing will give you confidence that you have selected the right long-term goals to enable your company to move forward successfully.

CHAPTER SUMMARY

What are Long-Term Goals?

They are objectives or milestones you aim to achieve within five years. They reflect your best estimates of the financial, operational, and other targets that you believe you can make in realistic terms.

Why are Long-Term Goals Important?

Clear and meaningful long-term goals help you create targets to aim for on the way to fulfilling your BSV and supporting your Brand Purpose. They motivate people and create higher levels of engagement as people feel challenged to achieve them.

NOTES

My ideas for our long-term goals include:

SIX

Conduct Session 1

TOTAL OF 6 HOURS

- **Brand Purpose—1 hour**
- **Values—1.5 hours**
- **Blue Sky Vision (10 Year)—1 hour**
- **SWOT Analysis—1.5 hours**
- **Long-Term (5 Year) Goals—1 hour**

In advance of the meeting, we recommend that you:

1. Identify the members of the team.
2. Provide every team member their own copy of this book.
3. Ask them to read the Session 1 section and come to the meeting with their own ideas.
4. Complete any necessary employee and customer surveys that are useful for the leadership elements of your plan and distribute the results to your team in advance of the meeting.
5. Set a time and place for the meeting when all team members can meet, preferably in person.

Instructions for Conducting the Meeting

Gather your team into a comfortable meeting room. You could go offsite for this first meeting to ensure people are not interrupted or distracted with phone calls or emails. Ask everyone to give their full and undivided attention to the meeting. Allow your team members to offer their own ideas about each item in the session. If you are the CEO or President, avoid going into the meeting with preconceived ideas that you insist everyone accept. Encourage their participation and the results will be much more collaborative. Let people speak from their heart, authentically, without any type of "business-speak" or jargon. Invite creativity and heartfelt expressions into the meeting.

Go through, one by one, the four Leadership components (Brand Purpose, Values, Blue Sky Vision, and SWOT) and one of the Management components (long-term goals) of the plan as suggested below. Consult the employee and customer surveys as needed. It's fine if you cannot nail down all the wordings perfectly in Session 1. Don't kill the momentum your team might have by trying to overly wordsmith their answers. Get some first impressions of wordings and allow them to ruminate among the group. It may take until Session 3 when you review Sessions 1 and 2 for great wording to suddenly appear through the creative process.

If you are unsure of which Brand Purpose, Blue Sky Vision, or five Values are going to be ultimately selected, we recommend you enter everything online at <u>LeadWithPurpose.com</u>. You will have access to all entries in the Leadership section, but only the top Brand Purpose, top BSV, and top five Values will show up when you view or print out your plan.

The information you put on the plan needs to be very succinct. If it is too long, it will not fit on the page, but more importantly it will be harder for you to explain and for people to understand and remember. Try to think of the headline of a newspaper article. For the Brand Purpose, Blue Sky Vision, and each of the Values, we provide a space for your shorter headline and a space right below it where you may add more detail. The image below shows this concept for the Brand Purpose.

Brand Purpose

1. Write each team member's ideas for your Brand Purpose on the board.
2. Make the statements as succinct as possible—5 to 10 words.
3. Potentially combine parts of different statements together.
4. Vote and choose the top one.
5. Refine the wording, but don't aim to perfect it in this session.
6. Enter your Brand Purpose in the Leadership tab of your plan online at <u>www.LeadWithPurpose.com</u>

Values

1. Have team members contribute their ideas for values. Write them on the board. If you want help with finding values, go to the resources section of <u>www.LeadWithPurpose.com</u> where you will find a list of the top 50 values.
2. Combine like items into groups and select a header for each group.
3. Vote on the groups to prioritize them from most to least relevant.
4. Select the top 5 values from among the groups.
5. Enter your values in the Leadership tab of your plan online at <u>www.LeadWithPurpose.com</u>

Blue Sky Vision

1. Determine what the company looks like in 10 years and what major goal has been accomplished.
2. Write different BSVs on the board.
3. Look to create a headline that describes your BSV.
4. Vote and choose the top one.
5. Refine the phrasing as needed, but don't aim for perfection in this session.
6. Enter your BSV into the Leadership tab of your plan online at www.LeadWithPurpose.com

SWOT

1. Using the blank template in the reading, perform a SWOT analysis on your company.
2. Write all the strengths on a board.
3. Combine like items and select group headers.
4. Vote to select the top three strengths.
5. Repeat steps 1-4 for weaknesses, opportunities, and threats.
6. Enter your SWOT into the Leadership tab of your plan online at www.LeadWithPurpose.com
7. Discuss the ancillary questions relevant to your responses on the SWOT:
- What resources do you need and what are the activities you need to keep doing to maintain your strength position?
- What resources do you need and what activities do you need to do to remove each weakness from this list?
- What do you need to do to counter a weakness that your competitors and customers are aware of?
- Do any of your internal strengths help you take advantage of the opportunities identified?
- What do you need to do and what resources do you need to reduce a threat?
- Do you have any strengths that could help you reduce a threat?

1. Create three long-term goals for your company.
2. See if they support your BSV and if not, refine them further.
3. Discuss a general action plan and identify resources and potential obstacles
4. Apply the SMART Method to ensure they are clear and meaningful.
5. Enter your long-term goals in the Management tab of your plan online at www.LeadWithPurpose.com.
6. For each long-term goal you have, fill in the Goal Name, a Detailed Description, an Action Plan, and the Potential Obstacles.

***

You are now done with Session 1. It is important that you summarize the information immediately and get it back out to every team member (by either giving them access to the site or printing it out as a PDF). They will need this information so they can work on their goals and be ready to come to Session 2.

Ask your team members to review the chapters in the next section in preparation for Session 2. Encourage them to get their employees' input and involvement in the creation of the annual and quarterly goals. Start sharing the plan immediately.

Allow 1 week between sessions.

SESSION 2

COMPLETING THE
MANAGEMENT ELEMENTS

SEVEN

Establishing Annual and Quarterly Goals

A good journey starts with knowing your final destination and then working backwards to understand the milestones to get there. If your long-term goals represent such a five-year journey, then your immediate one-year goals and current quarterly goals reflect the intermediate mileposts. They are the stops along the way to your destination. If you fail to stay on course and reach these stops, you might not make it.

It's like planning for a trip from Los Angeles to Chicago on the famous Route 66. You know where you are starting and your final destination. To go from A to B, you need to make stops in many cities along the way. Making advance plans allows you to calculate your schedule, budgets, and daily activities. You may hit some inclement weather, or take some detours, but for the most part, you make every effort to stay on Route 66 and reach your goal.

It is the same process with goal setting for the coming year and the current quarter. You have a long-term goal and you know you need to make it to that destination. Your short-term annual and quarterly goals are the equivalent of the stops along the way. These goals help you plan the company's operations, budgets, employment numbers, training, equipment, supply needs, and more. Changing course will have a big impact on the company, so the short-term goals help you stay on the path to the final destination.

By doing it this way, you give your organization the best opportunity to be successful because you spell out for employees exactly how their daily activities link up to the bigger picture. They can see how their current quarterly goals support the annual goals, which progressively move the company towards its long-term goals, which is how the organization reaches its Blue Sky Vision. When employees see this linkage, they understand how important their jobs are. They can trace on the plan how their efforts directly make or break the company's survival. As a result, they tend to become more engaged, committed, and willing to go the extra mile.

How to Formulate Annual and Quarterly Goals

This process is highly dependent on your company and the members of your team, as it is a function of how many departments are involved and how many goals you want to identify. This is why it is useful for your team to have a week before Session 2 happens. They can read this chapter and then share the results of the first session with the various departments they are responsible for and get their input on the annual and quarterly goals.

When you meet in Session 2, give each member 20 minutes to present their annual and quarterly goals to the team. Write these goals on the white board or easel. Have the entire team prioritize the top three annual goals for each of the long-term goals. Then, for each annual goal, you can collectively select the most appropriate quarterly goals.

Be sure to identify what department is responsible for the goal, the timeframe for completion, the action plan to achieve it, and any obstacles that might be encountered. The resources section at www.LeadWithPurpose.com has some forms that team members might find useful in helping them think through and organize their annual and quarterly goals.

The Advantages of Using Our Platform

If you use www.LeadWithPurpose.com, the long-term goals have already been entered, but it is also easy to record and keep track of your annual and quarterly goals using many features we have provided:

- *Annual goals.* Although you can create any number of annual goals, we recommend you have no more than seven. You record annual goals by attaching them as sub-goals to specific long-term goals, which helps you link the two to ensure that each annual goal supports a long-term goal.

- *Quarterly goals.* For each annual goal, you can attach any number of quarterly goals. You attach them as sub-goals to specific annual goals, which helps you link the two closely to ensure each quarterly goal supports an annual one.

For every goal you create, whether it is an annual or quarterly, you can add this information:

- *Name the goal.* Give the goal a name in plain English
- *Detailed description.* You can add a brief description of the goal
- *Action Plan.* You can write out an action plan along with tasks you need to complete.
- *Potential obstacles.* You can enter the potential barriers that might interfere with achieving the goal.
- *Assign the goal to a department.* You can choose the department from a drop-down list.
- *Status.* You can choose the goal's status from a drop-down list: On Track, At Risk, Unknown, Critical, and Completed.
- *Expected date.* You can identify the intended date of completion.
- *Completion date.* You can enter the actual date of completion.

There are three significant benefits of using our platform.

- *Achieving Total Alignment.* Online, you can't create a quarterly goal unless it is attached under an annual goal and every annual goal is connected under one of your long-term goals. All of the long-term goals support reaching your inspiring Blue Sky Vision which helps you to fulfill your Brand Purpose.

- *Flexibility to modify.* In today's world, companies need to be agile. Things are constantly shifting—competition, markets, new technologies, and so on. Companies often need to adjust their planning on the fly, even as immediate as their current quarterly goals. Using our system makes it very easy to revise or update your goals. You can easily add new ones, delete some, or change the action plan behind one of them, adjust the list of obstacles, or modify the intended completion date and status. This capability is hard to do without an automated system such as ours.

• *Instant Notification.* Any time someone makes a change to the plan, our system sends an email to all team members who have been authorized to use the system. This helps the team stay abreast of changes and see any modifications that might affect their own goals.

In general we use a tree structure to show all of the supporting goals and how they are aligned. Below is how it looks online in the Management section with one long-term, one annual goal, and three quarterly goals.

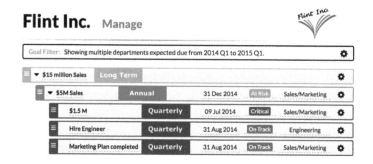

CHAPTER SUMMARY

What are Annual and Quarterly Goals?

These are the specific targets you aim to reach within one year and within the current period of 90 days. Setting these goals is critical to ensuring you are on the path to your longer-range goals, including your long-term (five-year) goals and your Blue Sky Vision.

Why are Annual and Quarterly Goals Important?

These goals are the most immediate goals that you want to hold people accountable for in their jobs. These goals clarify what people need to do, give them targets to reach, and help them focus on what matters most.

NOTES

My ideas for our company's annual and quarterly goals include:

EIGHT

Conduct Session 2

THE MANAGEMENT ELEMENTS

TOTAL OF 3—4 HOURS

- **Annual Goal—1 hour**
- **Current Quarterly 90 Day Goals—1-2 hours depending on how many teams are developing quarterly goals**

Instructions in Advance of Meeting

1. Ask everyone to read the chapters in the Session 2 section of this book. Make sure they have the information that was completed in Session 1.

2. Look at the resources section at www.LeadWithPurpose.com for information and materials that might be useful to the team in creating annual and quarterly goals.

3. Have your team members prepare any information needed concerning their own annual and quarterly goals. They should review the long-term goals established in Session 1. If necessary, ask them to consult with any other employees whose input is needed regarding their annual and quarterly goals.

4. Set a time and place for the meeting when all team members you have selected can meet. This meeting can take place either in person or virtually.

Instructions for Conducting the Meeting

1. Begin by writing your three long-term goals across the top of a whiteboard.

2. Ask members to identify annual goals that link up with the long-term goals selected. Write each annual goal directly under the long-term goal it is associated with.

3. Vote on up to three annual goals for each long-term goal you have. Be sure to think about how the annual goals link to the long-term goal. If a long-term goal will not be worked on until two years out, do not feel the need to add annual or quarterly goals under it.

4. Next, under the annual goals, write each department heading on the board. For each annual goal, identify three to five appropriate current quarterly goals that are needed to support that annual goal. Write each quarterly goal under the department that is responsible for completing the goal. Unless a goal needs to be completed by a specific date, we recommend you set the date to the end of the period you are planning for.

5. Have each department review the quarterly and annual goals to ensure that nothing has been missed among the departments.

6. Log into www.LeadWithPurpose.com and enter your annual and quarterly goals online under the appropriate long-term goals that were established in Session 1. For each annual and quarterly goal you can fill in a Detailed Description of the goal, an Action Plan, and Potential Obstacles.

You are now done with Session 2. It is important that you summarize the information immediately and get it back out to every team member (by either giving them access to the site or printing it out as a PDF). They will need this information so they can be ready to come to Session 3. Ask your team members to review the chapters in the next section in preparation for Session 3.

Allow 1 week between sessions.

SESSION 3

FINALIZING YOUR ONE-PAGE PLAN

NINE

Review and Finalize Your Plan

Most every document improves with thinking and a second review. Your one-page plan is no different. Give team members a week to let the plan percolate in their subconscious mind where creative thinking happens. Consider these questions as everyone reviews the draft plan.

- *Brand Purpose.* Is it powerful, engaging, and meaningful, and demonstrates how your company is making a difference? Is it exciting to existing employees and will it attract the "A players" who share your passion? Will it transform your customers into loyal fans? Is it a statement that will be just as relevant 50 years from now?

- *Values.* Are they unique to your company? Do they represent the values you can live by at all times, even when the going gets tough?

- *Blue Sky Vision.* Does it describe how your company looks in ten years? Will it stretch the organization to achieve a really big goal? Is it inspiring to employees and potential employees?

- *SWOT.* Is your assessment accurate and complete? Has it helped you draw any inferences to target new opportunities or defend against competitors?

- *Long-term goals.* Do they stretch your company for five years, while being reasonable, actionable, and aligned with your Blue Sky Vision? Did you apply the SMART check to them to ensure they are meaningful and correctly stated?

- *Annual and quarterly goals.* Do they support your long-term goals? Did you apply the SMART method to check them and ensure they are valid?

Go through the plan in your Session 3 meeting and come to agreement on the final language you want each component to have. This is not meant to be an entire rehashing of the work that has already been done. Take up to an hour to discuss the plan and address any major issues people have. Remember that your plan will continue to evolve over time, and you can return to improve the phrasing as you have new insights or the conditions change. But keep in mind that while you do not want to continually change the annual and quarterly goals, there will be times when they need to be changed. A competitor might enter or leave the market so new goals might take priority as situations arise. This is the beauty of using the online platform. You can stay agile on the management items immediately ahead of you while keeping steadfast to longer-term leadership goals.

TEN

Add Symbols to Your Plan

Images tend to evoke strong memories and emotional reactions in people. This is why we believe that it is valuable to add a small symbolic or representative image to the three top Leadership components of your plan: Brand Purpose, Values, and Blue Sky Vision. Such images are powerful messaging tools for most people— think of the saying, *"A picture is worth a thousand words."*

Academic research supports an overwhelming preference among humans for visual communication. A study by New York University psychologist Jerome Bruner showed that people remember 10% of what they hear, 20% of what they read, and 80% of what they see. [4]

Using images also helps people who process information differently than written text. Some people are verbal and word oriented, while others are picture-oriented. Using symbols thus allows you to appeal to both types.

Consider this. If I wrote a sentence about the tragedy of 9/11 and the terrible loss of life, it would certainly make you recall the event in your mind's eye. But if I showed you a photo of the World Trade Center building being hit by an airplane or crumbling down, you'd definitely experience a deep sense of shock and sadness.

Here's an example of the power of images to evoke specific concepts. Look at the image of the hammer, nails, and pieces of wood here. What do you associate with this image?

You might be thinking of someone building a house or a fence.

Now take a look at the hammer, nails, and wood in this second image. What do you think of now?

You probably recognize this being connected to the Christian religion. For over two billion Christians in the world today, this is a powerful symbol of their religion and reflects the core of Christian beliefs about Jesus. For them, a hammer, some nails, and two pieces of wood translate into an entire doctrine and philosophy of life based on faith, love, and hope.

These symbols are *evocative* and *emotional* reminders of stories about Jesus that have been told to millions of people over the millennia. This is just one example, as all religions use symbols to represent and reinforce their messages.

Companies can equally use images with emotional power to motivate and inspire both employees and customers. In the advertising world, we are all familiar with the many well-known logos and images reflecting the world's most famous brands. Think of the Nike swoosh, the Disney castle, and the Pillsbury doughboy—and you immediately experience an emotional link or a strong feeling about the company's brand.

As you finalize the Leadership components of your plan, now is the time to select and assign images to symbolize the phrasings you have created. There are many online sites where you can find images to use for free, but be sure not to copy an image that is copyrighted without paying its fee.

If you are using our web platform, www.LeadWithPurpose.com, you can choose from our Symblicity™ Library of over 600 images. We have categorized these images according to key words, so simply search a term that you want to associate with and you will most likely find many corresponding images. For instance, if you use "integrity" as one of your values, you will find dozens of images in our library associated with that word. If you do not find a symbol you like in our library, you can upload one and either keep it private for your own use or share it with the rest of the community using the platform.

When you print your plan using our web site, the symbols you have chosen will automatically appear. This way, your plan displays both your wording and the associated images for Brand Purpose, Values, and Blue Sky Vision.

Here are some examples of a definition and an image chosen for the five Values of a company.

HEADLINE	DESCRIPTION	IMAGE
Making A Difference	We strive for excellence and make a difference in the lives of our customers and fellow employees. We are excited about the products we make that positively affect peoples lives.	
Customer First	We strive to meet and exceed the needs of the customer. We always put the customer first.	
Innovative	We collaborate with each other and the customer to try to find the best possible solution for the challenge that is in front of us. We think outside the box and provide innovative solutions.	
Honesty	We work with honesty and integrity when we interact with each other and with our customers.	
Nimble	We understand that the environment we work in is constantly changing and that we need to be able to accept changes, adapt, and be flexible.	

ELEVEN

Conduct Session 3

ESTIMATED TIME—3 HOURS

- **Review Plan—1 hour**
- **Select Symbols —2 hour**

Instructions in Advance of Meeting

1. Print out and distribute copies of your finalized one-page plan.

2. Ask everyone to read the chapters in the Session 3 and review the entire plan for completeness.

3. Reviewing the Brand Purpose, Values, and Blue Sky Vision, have people think through the images that come to mind when they think of these leadership components. Bring images or a list of images to the session.

Instructions for Conducting the Meeting

1. Go around the table with your team and confirm that everyone accepts and buys into the wordings you have created so far. Revise any phrasings as necessary.

2. On the whiteboard or easel, draw a grid like the one shown here and write down your Brand Purpose, Values, and Blue Sky Vision headlines. Then explain each one in a few short sentences and think of some key words that might be used to search online for an image that represents your idea.

COMPONENT	HEADLINE	DETAILED DESCRIPTION	KEY WORDS TO FIND A CORRESPONDING IMAGE
Brand Purpose			
Value 1			
Value 2			
Insert more rows for additional values			
Blue Sky Vision			

3. Using www.LeadWithPurpose.com, click on each of the Leadership components that you have already filled out. To the left of the headline, you will see a link to "Choose symbol." From here you can either search symbols in the Symblicity Library matching your keywords, or upload your own symbol.

If the images don't feel exactly right, don't feel rushed to pick them immediately in this meeting. One other fun activity we have seen companies do to facilitate the image selection process is to involve the entire company. Put the Brand Purpose, Blue Sky Vision, and each of the Values on a wall. Next, tell everyone they have one week to put images on the wall that represent what those phrases and words mean to them. After one week, number the images and have people vote on the top ones. In the end, you should have seven images total: one for your Brand Purpose, one for your Blue Sky Vision, and five for the five Values.

4. Set the date to roll the plan out to the enter company. For some companies, it will be important to translate so everyone can fully understand.

You are now done with Session 3. Please summarize the notes and make any revisions that were discussed. Enter the images online and then distribute the updated plan to the entire team.

Your next step is to communicate this new plan to the entire company at every level. Read on to learn how to do this and learn the 7 principles that are key to successfully implementing your plan throughout your organization.

***

TWELVE

Rolling Out Your One-Page Plan

We shared with you earlier in the book that you will be able to use your one-page plan to get everyone on the same page, passionate about what they are doing, and focused on what matters most. To achieve this. you need to communicate your plan to the entire company at every level, amplifying the long-term inspiring story while clearly defining for everyone what their specific role is short-term. Gather everyone together at an all-hands meeting where you can walk through each of the different rungs of your ladder. This meeting should be no longer than 45 minutes, leaving as much time as necessary for employee questions.

It is best to explain each of the components in the order they were laid out in this book. Teach everyone what the component is and why it is important by using the summaries provided at the end of each chapter. Then share a quick story that will help them visualize and remember what you said.

Here is an example of how one after-school day care center shared its newly created Brand Purpose "Creating Confident and Socially Responsible Humans."

What it is? I want to share with you our new Brand Purpose. A Brand Purpose is a simple and memorable statement that describes the reason we exist and the difference our programs make in the world. It is also the promise we deliver relative to our customer expectations.

Why is it Important? You might be asking why a Brand Purpose is important. It is important because if you clearly understand the difference we are making in the world, we believe that you will be really inspired about where you spend eight hours of your day. We want you to feel that your work is relevant and that what you do is important. Having a great Brand Purpose has been shown to increase employee engagement and customer loyalty.

Our Brand Purpose. Our new Brand Purpose is "Creating Confident and Socially Responsible Humans." We looked at the programs we provide for families and their children and we kept asking "Why Does That Matter?" In summary, all of our afterschool programs have a purpose. Whether it is story time, or drawing, or free play, we are teaching children life's lessons and building their character and confidence.

Our Stories. Think of all of the children whom you have had the opportunity to form and mold. Think of how shy and hesitant Billy was when he came to us two years ago. Think of his transformation over the last two years. Now, he looks you in the eye when he talks to you and is willing to try new things and is not so worried about failing. Think of all the confident and socially responsible people you have developed.

Our Symbol. We looked at many different symbols and chose the following symbol to represent our Brand Purpose. Just as a young sapling needs nurturing hands to help it grow to be strong, we are the hands that help nurture young children to be confident and socially responsible human beings.

That is how easy it is. Follow the same steps with each of the other Leadership elements. There are no symbols for the SWOT Analysis. For your Blue Sky Vision, it is best to share with everyone the details of what the company looks like in ten years. Then share your Blue Sky Vision headline that was chosen to succinctly represent the envisioned future.

Next, detail the long-term, annual, and quarterly goals and show their alignment to the Blue Sky Vision and Brand Purpose. Close this section by stating the obvious, which is that every quarterly goal an employee works on connects to your Brand Purpose.

The meeting will be successful if everyone walks away having an understanding of the overall big picture story, what they need focus on in the next 90 days, and how what they are doing connects to making a difference in the world. They should also know that you are committed to the plan and making it work.

7 PRINCIPLES
TO IMPLEMENT
YOUR PLAN

You and your team invested a significant amount of time and energy crafting your unique story and determining the values that are important to the culture. You worked backwards to create your ladder to the envisioned future, detailing the shorter term goals people need to work on and how they connect to the big picture.

Creating a plan and dreaming about the future is a lot of fun, but the real value comes when you begin implementing your plan and find that you achieve greater success than you ever have before. The fact is, an *Economist* magazine report cited that 61% of senior executives acknowledge that their firms often struggle to bridge the gap between strategy formulation and its day-to-day implementation.[5] Developing a strategy is one thing, but implementing is another. As Vince Lombardi said, "The best game plan in the world never blocked or tackled anyone." No matter how good your plan is, if you cannot put it into action and implement it correctly, it is not worth the paper it is written on.

There are two critical advantages that a one-page plan helps you with that can prevent such a failure as you try to implement your new strategy.

First, the limited space on a single page forced you to be succinct and prioritize what is most important. There aren't 30+ pages to thumb through and confuse people. Everything sits on a single page which makes it easy for you to explain and, more importantly, easy for everyone to look at and understand.

Second, you have involved your team in the formation of the plan. People who have had a hand in developing any plan and its goals have a higher level of buy-in and will work harder to make it come true.

While having it all on a single page and getting employees involved is a great start to implementing your newly created plan, the most value comes in having more than just a few of the team members engaged. To make this happen we provide you with the following seven additional principles.

PRINCIPLE 1

Own The Plan

The single most important factor of whether any plan will succeed is having a champion who owns the plan. As the President or CEO, you can't be too busy for this and you can't push this responsibility off to other employees. As the leader, you are the person who needs to own and drive the plan.

In the past, if you have jumped on the latest management fad of the month, your employees may be rolling their eyes. They will be thinking of the last time they wasted a lot of time sitting in meetings, learning new buzz words, or forming cross-functional teams that ultimately produced nothing.

If you don't give your full commitment, employees will feel misled. Having a Brand Purpose, Blue Sky Vision, Values, SWOT, and some goals that aren't used will demoralize employees, especially those who were involved in its creation.

So what is the best way for you to show your executive team and employees that you own the plan and that is important to you? I draw upon a parenting quote from author James A. Baldwin who said, "Children have never been very good at listening to their elders, but they have never failed to imitate them."

It is the same with your employees. Your actions will speak louder than your words. They heard you roll out the plan. Now, everyone, including the team members who helped put the plan together, is watching you and your actions. They want to see that you are going to walk the talk. They will imitate what they see you do.

So what can you do?

Know The Plan

Commit to learning the plan inside and out. Don't be intimidated by this. It is a single page and is actually easier than it might sound. If you spend 10 minutes every morning reviewing your plan, it will take you approximately 2-3 weeks to know it thoroughly.

Knowing your plan allows you to have conversations with your executive team and employees about it. If your people hear you say that your five values are important, you will render the entire plan less valuable in everyone's eyes if later on you stumble through or forget one. Don't have your employees asking themselves "He says this is important, but how important can it be? He doesn't even know them."

To start, memorize your Brand Purpose, five Values, and Blue Sky Vision. There are symbols associated these components to help you remember them. Next, memorize your top Strength, Weakness, Opportunity, and Threat and your three long-term goals. Then, memorize the 5-7 annual company goals in order of importance. Finally, become familiar with all of quarterly goals and reference your plan to remind you exactly what each one is. You can get to know the plan alone or you can go through this together with your management team. Either way, expect everyone on the management team to know the plan also.

Start Using It Immediately

Print out a copy for yourself or use your tablet or smart phone to have access to the plan at all times. Print copies for other team members or give them access online. Carry it everywhere you go and encourage others leaders to do the same. Reference the plan as you address the different leadership and management challenges the company faces daily. Urge team members to bring a copy of the plan to all of their meetings and use it in front of their employees. Make updates to the plan online as necessary. When you do, everyone connected online to the plan will receive an email with your update showing them that you are using it.

Review Your Plan Regularly

Having plan review meetings on a consistent and regular basis shows by action that the plan is important. Make it part of your routine and put a plan review into your schedule, as follows:

- *Weekly.* Review the plan briefly each week with your leadership team, focusing only on what might need further clarification. Update the action items and obstacles as necessary. Are the expected due dates still realistic and on track? Does anyone need help on a goal?

- *Monthly.* Spend 15 minutes updating the entire company. Celebrate what has been completed and review what still needs to get done that quarter. Ask people to identify where they need help to overcome an obstacle. Share stories of how employees are living the Brand Purpose, Blue Sky Vision, or the Values.

- *Quarterly.* Set aside two hours to revisit your plan every 90 days and have your leadership team update their quarterly goals as you move into the next quarter. Share stories of how employees are living the Brand Purpose, Blue Sky Vision, or the Values. Update the SWOT with any changes. Finally, have each person present to the rest of the team what they accomplished the last 90 days and what will be focused on in the upcoming quarter. Communicate the plan with the entire company.

- *Annually.* Conduct an annual meeting with your leadership team to assess the status of your current annual goals and to update your plan for the coming year's annual and first quarter goals. This is also a time to check on whether your company is on the path to fulfilling your long-term goals and the Blue Sky Vision. Spend 30 minutes sharing the results of this meeting with the entire company.

Using a one-page plan makes it easy, uncomplicated, and non--threatening to do strategic planning on a regular basis, especially if you are using our online tools. Regularly reviewing the plan with the team provides transparency on those things that are most important and that transparency helps to build trust.

If you have ever done traditional strategic planning or hired a consultant to do it for you, you know that it can be an enormous drain on your time and money to create or annually update a 20 or 30 page document that ultimately sits on a shelf. If you do it yourself, it is reduced to days. If you need or want support in the process, we have certified *Lead With Purpose* coaches who can assist you in the strategic thinking and creation of your one-page plan at a fraction of the cost of traditional planning.

By knowing it, using it, and scheduling regular reviews, your actions will reinforce your words that the plan is important. Employees will see this and start imitating your actions and eventually become owners of the plan also.

PRINCIPLE 2

Own The Culture

One of the most important expressions about leadership that I have heard is that "the CEO owns the culture." While this could fall under the *Own the Plan principle*, we felt it was so important that it deserved to be its own principle. We are not alone. Peter Thiel, the cofounder of PayPal and early investor of Facebook, invested $150 M in Airbnb in 2012. Brian Chesky, CEO of Airbnb, asked his new investor what the single most important piece of advice he had.

Thiel's response was, *"Don't f*ck up the culture."*

Chesky was surprised at this reply, so he asked for clarification. Thiel explained that the current culture was one of the reasons he invested in the company and he was concerned that when the company grew, it would lose its culture. He wanted Chesky to keep a strong eye on the culture.

If you are the head of your company, or on its leadership team, the one-page plan gives you an opportunity to remake or reinvigorate your culture and transform your company in significant ways. As you go about implementing your plan, you have the chance to lay a strong new foundation on which to build your future.

Think about it. You and your team have spent weeks of time and energy selecting your Brand Purpose, Values, Blue Sky Vision, and long-term goals. You've done the SWOT assessment and can take action more intelligently based on your strengths, weaknesses, opportunities and threats. You received input from the team regarding their annual and quarterly goals. In short, you have everything you need to crystalize your organizational culture around the plan.

Having a strong culture built around a clear message and a sense of making a difference in the world is vital in growing organizations. It helps you attract the right people who share your passion and identify with your inspiring company story. It keeps people focused on what matters most and reduces internal competition and the silo mentality that often develops in larger companies with many departments that do not communicate or collaborate.

I've seen many companies grow in size and lose control of their culture. It often happens in small businesses that start out with a CEO and a handful of people who share the same passion for the product or service they produce. With only five or ten employees, the CEO and top executives know everyone. Since the company is small, the few employees who work there know their connection to their greater purpose. During these early days of the company, the owner knows every employee, where they went to college, who their favorite football team is, their spouse's name, how many kids they have, and even what they like in their coffee. It is a culture where everyone gets along and works closely together to reach their goals and overcome obstacles.

What happens though when the company grows beyond about twenty-five employees is that the owner can no longer maintain direct interaction with everyone. As the company expands, more people join from different backgrounds, bringing with them different experiences and values that can change the culture. The owner's hold on the company's culture lapses. Employees begin to lose sight of the company's Brand Purpose, Values, and Blue Sky Vision. This is the slippery slope down to having serious problems with employee engagement. Workers can begin to think of the company as just a job, or a stepping stone to a better job elsewhere.

One of the most significant impacts on developing your culture is the degree to which employees willingly adopt the company values. When your values are widely disseminated, people look to them for guidance in their daily interactions and activities. This reduces the risk of someone going against the values—because when that happens, it sets a bad example and other values lose their credibility. Indeed, the biggest test of values comes not when your company is doing well, but when the business is struggling and there are challenging decisions to make. Make sure your employees will not bend the values during these times. One of my favorite quotes comes from Roy Disney, who said, *"When your values are clear to you, making decisions becomes clearer."*

So what can you do?

Human Resources Activities

Use your HR department to amplify your plan through their key activities.

- When interviewing new hires, talk about your Brand Purpose, Values, and Blue Sky Vision. Share with them real stories of how employees have treated each other and customers and assess how candidates react. Do they seem to share that passion? One company changed its hiring forms to ask questions relating to its values. "It is so easy right now to see who fits in culturally and who doesn't," said its HR Director.

- Integrate the plan into your employee performance reviews and job promotion process. Assess employees not only on how well they fared in meeting their quarterly goals, but also on their attitudes and behaviors relative to the company values.

- Conduct training sessions to educate current and future employees on the meaning of the plan components to ensure they understand how each component relates directly to them.

Incorporating your one-page plan into these key HR activities creates a virtuous spiral. The more you hire and build a workforce that resonates with your plan, the stronger your culture will become. A strong culture then attracts more employees who share your passion.

Encourage Storytelling

Storytelling has been used since the earliest times and is the fabric upon which many cultures have been built. Stories create engagement beyond a level of intellectual understanding as they build an emotional resonance with employees and customers. Many companies are turning to storytelling to transform their vision and message into exciting, compelling, and entertaining formats. One key way to do this is to turn your employees and customers into the heroes of the stories.

Here is an example of how Caseworx uses storytelling to amplify their Brand Purpose and strengthen their culture. Caseworx designs and manufactures custom cabinets that transform universities, commercial properties, and high-end residential homes. Using *Lead With Purpose,* they were able to generate their Brand Purpose which is "We Craft Inspiring Spaces." The company leadership started gathering pictures of their customer's finished spaces and hung them on a "Wall of Fame" they created in the manufacturing plant. Now, instead of just knowing the job as Getty, they could see how their product transformed the Getty Museum in Los Angeles. Starting with the pieces of wood that were cut to proper size to the holes drilled to adding the hardware to the assembly of the cabinet, for every employee who touched this job, the image of the room at the Getty Museum brought their work to life.

Monthly, the entire company meets to share stories and recognize employees who are "Crafting Inspiring Spaces" and living the values. Caseworx President Gregg Schneider adds, "We want our employees to feel proud about the work they do. We have always produced high-quality cabinets, but the Brand Purpose and the succinct set of values helped us to elevate how we view ourselves. Now, instead of just feeling like we are wood workers, we see ourselves as craftsmen who help to transform some of the most recognizable buildings in the United States."

Schneider adds "We meet monthly in the plant in front of a large image of our one-page plan on the wall. I stand in front of this and use it to help tell our story and then recognize employees for living our Brand Purpose and our five values. It is simple to do and very effective."

You can create stories around any of the following topics:

- What is the reason your company exists and the difference it makes in the world?
- What are its leaders passionate about accomplishing?
- Why do customers love and value your product or service?
- Why are employees highly engaged and excited about being a part of the culture?
- What values does your company live by and want the world to respect you for?

As your stories are created, promote them everywhere. In today's world, it's easy to disseminate your stories in many communication channels, including the countless social media platforms such as Facebook, Twitter, YouTube, Yelp, and Pinterest. Many companies even encourage their employees and customers to create and share stories in the form of videos and images that contribute to a company's brand authenticity.

Formal Speeches and Informal Chats

Some leaders are great at public speaking, others don't do so well. Your one-page plan gives you everything you need to run monthly, quarterly, and annual all-hands company meetings wherein you review the plan with all of the employees and show them your passion for it in person.

I know that many business owners and executives feel uncomfortable about speech making. I've heard a lot of them say things like "I am not very inspiring" or "My dad stood in front of everyone when he ran the company, but I can't do it" or "I am not a good motivator or public speaker." If you are among these leaders, don't worry. You don't need to be a professional motivational speaker. Just let your company's purpose inspire and motivate you to talk informally with your people.

Use the meeting schedule in Principle #1 as a guide for the formal meetings, but don't be afraid to informally bring the team together when you need to. The company might have just won an award, secured a new customer, or achieved a milestone, so bring everyone together and tell a story that acknowledges what was accomplished, recognizes which employees made it happen, and references how what they did is connected to your Brand Purpose, one of your Values, or your Blue Sky Vision.

Recognize and Reward Employees

Recognizing and rewarding employees whenever they go over and above their job description is another way to build your culture, especially if you do it as part of a concerted effort rather than just random acts or on a "If we remember to do it" basis.

One company I worked with, Active Mobility, created their plan and from it implemented a rewards system called "Catching you in the act of." Whenever they noticed an employee doing something in line with their values, such as delivering exceptional customer service, the employee was handed an "Active Mobility Bucks" in front of other employees. The rewards money stated "You're Acting World-Class" and could be exchanged for gift cards.

As Dr. Ron Cottrell, President of Active Mobility, shared: "The Active Mobility Bucks as a way to reward employees for practicing our values is brilliant and has been a huge hit with our employees. The symbols on the bucks that match the symbols around the office and on our one-page plan is locking the concepts into all of our minds!" He also added, "In the past, I would feel a lot of pressure to structure staff meetings, but now that our plan is in place, I am excited about the upcoming meetings and feel like they are much more interactive and fun."

As you migrate to using a one-page plan on a consistent basis, it is the perfect time to reclaim your company culture or reset its course. You and your team of leaders can become even more intentional about reinforcing and propagating the shared vision of the Brand Purpose and a set of Values that are clear, compelling, and exciting. Use your plan to rally the troops around a central focus of your culture.

PRINCIPLE 3

Stay Focused on What Matters Most

Passion, Product, Productivity, and Profits—these are what matter most in the majority of companies, no matter what size you are. Having a one-page plan makes it easier for you to pay attention to these four key factors of success, especially when you are consistently amplifying your message and teaching people how their work links up to support the big picture.

Passion. People want simple messages, to feel that they are part of something bigger, and to know they are making a difference in the world. When they get these, they tend to become more engaged in their work, experiencing greater energy and passion for what their company seeks to accomplish. In the majority of the companies where I took over as interim CEO, I witnessed that giving employees a clear understanding of how they make a difference was the most important driver fueling the company's turnaround. It was inspiring to see the exact same employees who had been failing before become catalysts for change, bringing the company back to stability and success.

I call making this linkage for employees the *Economics of Passion*. Once you inspire employees and fulfil their need for meaningful messages and a sense of making a difference in the world, you will be amazed at how you can impact the passion they bring to their work day in and day out. Employees fall in love with their work when they feel it is meaningful and relevant. When this occurs, their level of commitment rises and it can literally impact the bottom line.

Product. I know nothing about your specific business so I can't tell you how to make your product better. What I can assure you is that your product will improve significantly. Here is why. Passionate employees generally care more and are fueled by seeing how they have impacted the lives of their customers. The more stories, the better. Employees start asking customers how the product can be better. The market feedback is used to refine or add new functionality, which gets the product to additional customers, which produces more difference-making stories, which further engages your employees.

Productivity. The plan helps people become more productive because it shows them precisely how their work relates to the company's success all the way up the chain. Leadership can literally draw a line from what people do every day to achieve their department's quarterly goals, up to the company's annual goals, to its long-term goals, to its Blue Sky Vision, and ultimately to its Brand Purpose.

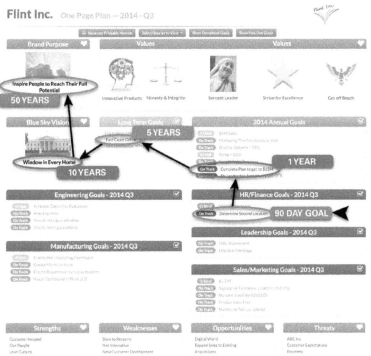

Profit. One valuable benefit of the plan, especially if you use our website, is its ability to track and link the status of your goals up and down the chain in order to gain a tighter control on your profitability. You begin by creating your long-term goals from which you build your annual goals to support them, and your quarterly goals to support the annual ones. All three levels are tightly intertwined.

With this information, it is much easier for a company to create a set of financials and an annual budget.

Then, as you conduct business, you can track the quarterly goals. You can clearly see if their status enables you to reach your annual goals and budget, and consequently, if the status of the annual goals puts you on the path to your long-term goals.

In short, your one-page plan gives you the ability to consistently monitor people's accountabilities up the chain and take action to improve situations as needed. This clarity of tracking and linking of goals provides companies with precisely the rigor and discipline they need to manage their annual budget and boost their profits.

So what can you do?

Make Sure Everyone Understands Their Ladder

As discussed in Principle #1, it is imperative that the leadership team knows and is fully committed to the plan. It would be outstanding if every other employee understood the entire plan, but that isn't initially realistic. To start, have people see how what they are doing connects to making a difference in the world. Let me give you an example of how to do this.

Calmont Wire & Cable, Inc. is a company that produces wire of all types and having been in business for more than fifty years, has a long tradition of solving complex engineering problems. Located in Southern California, its breakthrough came in 1960 when it was approached by Wham-o and became the first company to successfully manufacture the Hula Hoop with a stripe. Their company's wire products were also used on the first spacecraft to land on the moon, the Apollo 11. They produce wiring thin enough to be used in heart implant devices and durable enough to be used in complex military equipment. They also manufactured the world's first artificial wine cork.

In 2012, I arrived at Calmont as interim CEO. I was told that they had a manufacturing problem because of the large amount of product returns every month. I listened to their theory that the machines were outdated and they needed to manage the manufacturing process better. If I had accepted that as the root cause of their problems, I would have spent all my time asking questions about their equipment, processes, and procedures.

But I intuitively felt that something deeper was wrong. I began walking around the shop floor and simply asking questions to the machine operators about what they were doing. I walked over to one employee and asked him what he was producing. "Some wire," he told me. "What's it being used for?" I asked him. "I don't know," he replied. I turned to the VP of Operations and asked him to tell the operator what the wire was used for. "It goes in a medical device, a heart pacemaker." The machine operator was astonished. He had no idea that this very thin wire he was in charge of producing found its purpose in a heart device keeping someone alive. When he finally understood the importance of this wire, he realized that he had to monitor his machine much more closely to prevent flawed wire from being produced and shipped to the customer.

We walked over to another machine operator and asked the same question. He, too, had no idea that his wire was being used by the Defense Department in satellites. All the prior years, he only saw it as wire, not a critical electronic component of a multi-million dollar satellite that the U.S. counted on for our national protection. He began to understand how his job was of vital importance to the company and promised us that he would be more careful in assuring his output was precision made.

Within one month of this discovery, the company dropped from $25,000 per month in returned wire to less than $5,000—and has stayed at that level ever since. I did not have to implement any management retraining program, Six Sigma or Lean intervention, or purchase any new equipment. The problem turned out not to have anything to do with equipment, but rather to a disconnect between the employee and what he or she thought the job was about. In many ways, it was a failure of leadership to make sure the company's workers understood how their jobs linked up to the "big picture" of the company's Brand Purpose, its Values, and its Blue Sky Vision. The machine operators didn't understand the impact of what they were producing. Once they learned where their wire ended up—e.g., how what they were producing made a difference in the world—they started truly caring about their jobs.

This had a direct impact on the product, productivity, and profits of the company. Employees started managing their time and work efforts to make sure the wire was being produced right the first time. Time and money wasn't being spent on remaking wire. The product passed the customer's initial inspection. Profits increased.

One other valuable benefit of this approach is observing who is truly passionate about the difference your company makes. It is easy to see which people change their attitude and approach to work and those who don't. In the above example, the culture of making it right the first time turned many non-performers into valuable employees, but two remained apathetic and in-time left the company on their own.

I have had many experiences like this one in my career in which leaders were failing to focus on what matters most or to connect the dots about what their jobs were really about. As you begin implementing your plan, revisit any problems happening in your company, and you may be surprised with a more positive outcome.

Start with employees understanding how their bottom rung (quarterly goals) is linked to the top rung (Brand Purpose). They will be more engaged, which opens up the opportunity for you to discuss the other rungs of the ladder. You can see why it is so important in Principle #1 that the leadership team know the entire plan inside and out. Every interaction is an opportunity to help employees understand their own ladder and this directly impacts what matters most—Passion, Product, Productivity, and Profits.

Keep a Fanatical
Focus on Next Quarter

The long-term, annual, and quarterly goals are your well-thought out roadmap to achieving your Blue Sky Vision (10 years) and fulfilling your Brand Purpose. For each of the goals, you have been asked to think through an action plan and potential obstacles that you might encounter along the way. Now, the most important timeframe and focus where your team needs to spend almost all of their time, energy, and attention is on the upcoming quarter. You are probably wondering why.

Based upon our experiences and what we have seen, change is a challenge that every business has to deal with. Your annual goals were set based on assumptions made at the beginning of the year. For one annual goal, it could very well be that the first three of eight identified steps will be worked on in the first quarter. At this time you could also spend a significant amount of time detailing the remaining five steps that will occur after the first quarter is complete, but we recommend you wait to do that.

The famous Prussian General Carl Philipp Gottfried von Clausewitz stated it well by saying "No campaign plan survives the first contact with the enemy." It is the same with your plan. For any business, the customers and competitors won't act exactly how you expected them to or you may encounter other obstacles.

It is better that, at the end of any quarter, you evaluate what you accomplished and based upon what you now know, determine what the next steps are to complete the annual goal. The steps might still be the same original steps you identified, but they might be different.

If they have changed, the detailed planning you did at the beginning of the year will go to waste, but you will be better off revising your plan.

So what can you do?

Quarterly Visions

You and your management team need to create quarterly mini-visions. The script for this can be found in the quarterly boxes on your one-page plan. During the quarterly regularly scheduled meeting, discuss what was just accomplished, but with an eye on the annual goals, determine the upcoming set of quarterly goals. After the new quarterly goals for each department are presented, ask these questions to the entire team:

1. "If John's department completed these goals, would we consider that a good quarter?"
2. "Are the annual goals on track?"
3. "Is there anything missing or not prioritized correctly?"

Once all of the new quarterly goals have been presented and agreed upon, ask the same questions to the entire team. The updated plan then becomes the vision of what the team will have accomplished and where it expects to be in three months. A benefit of doing it this way is that the employees are the ones who put it together, so you have buy-in.

Everyone Knows Their Top 3

Every employee needs to "distinguish the vital few from the trivial many." This term was coined by the famous management consultant Dr. Joseph Juran. This requires giving employees the context to make these distinctions—and that context is found precisely in the plan. Go over the plan with them to ensure they understand it and know their top three quarterly goals from most to least important. This often helps employees begin to recognize what is important and what's not.

Defend Their Time and Attention

Employees today are inundated with distractions that interfere with their work. There are usually many little interruptions—a coworker stopping by the desk, a phone call, an email, a tweet, or a quick visit to their Facebook page—that keep people from staying focused. One study found that the average person is interrupted fifty-six times per day—that's once every 8 minutes.[6] The study found that 80% of those interruptions were unnecessary and that a person spends a total of two hours every day refocusing.

Another significant distraction results from just living in today's world—*information overload*. A University of California San Diego report states that Americans consume 34 gigabytes of data and 100,000 words daily. [7] This equates to viewing five hours of HD video and three times the total number of words in this book. As our brains fill with all of this data, we gradually lose the capability to concentrate fully.

You can eliminate distractions by asking employees to be cognizant of disruptions that take away their time. Many consultants suggest that social media sites like Twitter and Facebook and phone texting be banned at work. I have found that asking people simply to self-manage their online usage goes a long way to minimize distractions. I actually believe you have a bigger problem—lack of employee engagement—if you have to monitor people's Internet and social media usage at work.

Your one-page plan also helps you improve your own leadership role by reminding you to eliminate your own distractions and become more cognizant of trivial or irrelevant information crossing your desk. As Aimee Asebrook, President of SoCal Athletics said to me, "My one-page plan gives me permission not to pay attention to all the distractions in my life that are not high priority. If it isn't on my plan, it goes on the back burner until later."

Keep It to One-Page

In the same way that the most famous one-page documents of history—the 10 Commandments, the Magna Carta, the U.S.

Constitution, and others like these—there is something captivating about publishing a powerful, compelling, and meaningful message on a single page. Don't let the plan shift to two or more pages. The document will lose its effectiveness.

PRINCIPLE 5

Empower Employees
to be Responsive Decision Makers

Your one-page plan offers you an opportunity to empower your people and push decision making down to them. Having an empowered workforce is becoming a necessary part of running a successful business today. Here is why.

We live in a world where customers have great expectations from the companies they do business with. They don't want just a product or service; they want to have a relationship with your company. They want personalized service, not to be just a name on your books. Every employee needs to understand how to deliver on your company's brand. If you have the old command and control style set up where only a few at the top understand the brand and how to deliver, it will not work anymore.

In today's business environment, making sure your employees are responsive and able to meet, if not exceed, customer expectations is critical, especially in small companies. When consumers assess their customer satisfaction based on their buying experiences from world-class operations like Apple, Amazon, and Zappos, they will compare you based on that bar. When people can purchase nearly any book in the world from Amazon and have it delivered within 60 seconds to their computer or reading tablet, they begin to expect the same from everyone. When they can buy products online and get free 2-day shipping, they start to think that every retailer should be able to do so. When consumers have 365 days to return shoes they don't like to Zappos, no questions asked, it becomes like a "human right" everyone should provide. When consumers can practically demand "I need it better, cheaper, and faster and if I am not completely satisfied, I will tell everyone online instantly," you don't have much choice but to comply.

Your employees are your first line of ambassadors to your customers, suppliers, and other stakeholders. This reality has never been truer than today because technology increasingly links everyone together and connects your employees to the world as never before. Decades ago, if you had good service in a restaurant, you might tell 1, 2, maybe 5 people about it. Today, if people fall in love with a restaurant because of its food or great service, they blast their adoration out on Facebook, Twitter, Pinterest, Instagram, Yelp, and other online sites. But the same is true if people are dissatisfied with an experience they have with your company. And the lag time between bad service and a complaint is almost zero these days. People are quick to tweet or snap a photo with their cell phone and post it to the world within seconds. Even a single negative review can harm your reputation or cause the loss of future sales if it is credible, authentic, and persuasive to others who read it.

So what can you do?

Involve Employees in the Goal Setting

For each goal, allow people to think through the steps they will take, the resources they need, and any obstacles they might encounter. This will help them understand how their top 3 goals go from most to least important. People who have had a hand in creating their own goals are more engaged and have a vested interest in making sure the goals come true.

Give People a Framework to Be Owner of Their Business

Make people clearly aware that you are going to give them more responsibility and authority to make decisions. Because they have been involved in creating their own goals, they not only have a form of ownership, they also have a basic framework that they established themselves. If there are any other rules or guidelines, make sure they are simple to understand and see to it there are no gray areas. This could be the ability to resolve any customer issue less than $100 on the spot. It could be the ability to approve the hiring of certain employees without your signature or the freedom to purchase up to $500 of tools every month that help people be more productive. When I go into organizations, I am often amazed at the small level to which the President is still involved in decisions that his or her people can certainly make on their own, if given a chance.

Ask a Lot of Questions

There is a method called "guided discovery" that I recommend you learn more about. I was introduced to this concept while attending a week-long coaching course taught by US Soccer and reading a book by Lynn Kidman called *Developing Decision Makers: An Empowerment Approach to Coaching*. The book details the successes and challenges that Wayne Smith encountered when he became a coach of the New Zealand All Blacks rugby team.

When an employee comes to you with a problem, don't answer the question for them. Instead ask them a question back. "What do you think the solution is?" or "What factors do we need to take into account when evaluating what to do?" or "How have we handled this in the past?"

You have to resist the urge to answer the question for them. This is hard to do at first because we want to help, we have a certain way we want the problem solved, or we want to be seen as the expert. But it is a teaching moment if you ask employees to answer their own questions. If they can't answer it, ask them to do a little research and then come back for a follow-up conversation. When they return and say these are the potential solutions, don't make the decision for them; instead ask them what their recommendation is. Continue to ask questions and "guide" them to the right decision and then praise them. It will bolster their confidence and they will want to do it more.

If you begin practicing this guided discovery approach, employees will soon learn that you are going to ask them for their recommendations, and before they even come to you with a problem, they will go through these questions in their head so they are prepared. If they solve a problem with you guiding them and you believe they can solve this in the future on their own, tell them that you don't need to be involved next time.

Over time this process helps people gain a clearer understanding of what they are responsible for and the types of decisions they have authority and wisdom to make on their own. What happens next is that employees start solving problems on their own with little to no input from you. There are obvious big decisions that only you can make because of the importance or the speed with which the decision needs to be made, but as much as possible, begin answering a question with a question.

Start Small and Be Patient

Although you have told people you will be giving them more responsibility and asking more questions, people might not initially grasp what you are doing, so be patient as you set people up to be successful. Start with smaller decisions so people gain an understanding of the concept and they can earn some wins under their belt. This will build their confidence.

Always be patient with people. Do not ask questions in a sarcastic tone, as if they should know the answer. Do not respond to their answers negatively or judgmentally. Don't discount any of their ideas. Keep encouraging people to participate, such as: "That is a good thought, but what other ideas are there to solve the problem?" Remember that people will stumble in the beginning so it is your job to keep asking questions and encourage them to get to the right solution. For very simple decisions, let go of having to nitpick the solution. Let them retain ownership. Follow-up with them to ask how their solution is working and the impact it has had on them, your customers, or the business.

Think of this as similar to teaching someone how to drive. You put them in a safe situation on the back roads where there is less traffic and they can build their confidence. You progressively allow them to drive on the busier streets, then avenues, then freeways. You use your experience to warn them of potential issues, but you have to let them drive the car. Only in the most severe situations do you actually grab the wheel or pull the emergency brake.

These are some basic ideas of steps you can take to empower your people. What you should take from this principle is that, as leaders, we do a disservice to others if we don't allow them to reach their full potential. When we do something for them that they can and should do on their own, we take away their opportunity for learning and growth. Your employees can make the difference between staying in business—or going bust. The choice is yours. Do you want to empower them to take ownership of the role they play—or keep them in the dark and expect them just to follow orders without understanding the vision and inner workings of your company? Use your one-page plan to create a smart, proactive, customer-oriented workforce committed to your success.

PRINCIPLE 6

Remove Obstacles
that Block Employees

Once employees see the importance of their role, how it links all the way up the line to your Brand Purpose, and you have given them more responsibility to make decisions, it is your responsibility as a leader to enable them to step up to the plate and become all they can be. Now is the time to review all your operations to get rid of bureaucratic rules and useless procedures that prevent your employees from being able to make independent decisions to better serve customers and create positive experiences. Talk to employees and get their feedback on how they could become better equipped to participate in decisions. Given that you are investing time and energy to amplify your message, it serves no value to educate employees on your Brand Purpose, Values, Blue Sky Vision, and goals and then burden them with obstacles.

Use the Engage, Empower, and Encourage Leadership Approach

Tap into the Lead With Purpose "Engage, Empower, and Encourage" leadership approach to help your people reach their full potential. We strongly believe that human beings perform best when they are:

- *Engaged* in something they are passionate about.
- *Empowered* to take control and make decisions.
- *Encouraged* to strive for their goals and work through challenging times or failure.

Here's how you implement this approach.

Be Engaging. People fall in love with their work when they clearly understand how their company makes a difference and when they see how their values align with the company's culture. In conversations with your employees and customers, refer to the boxes designated with a red header and the heart to tell your story and engage people.

Be Empowering. People who are engaged in their work want to take more responsibility for their actions and treat the company as if it were their own. In Session 2, your employees thought through an action plan, required resources, and potential obstacles for each goal, so use their results now to pull yourself out of the day-to-day and push decision making down to them. Your conversations can shift now to focus on questions like: "How are you coming along on that goal?" "Are there any other resources you need?" You, in turn, can free yourself up to spend more time leading the company. The boxes in blue and designated with a check mark are what you will use to empower people, while holding them accountable.

Be Encouraging. Encourage your people to be the best they can be. Whenever you see great performance, recognize the person for living one of the company values or completing a goal. An encouraging word is one of the most effective things you can do to motivate people to continue pushing forward through any obstacles or failures. Use the recognition programs discussed in Key Principle #2 to reward the people you lead while strengthening your culture.

Every morning, take a few minutes to review the plan and renew your commitment to help people feel Engaged, Empowered, and Encouraged. Carry the plan with you throughout the day and reference it as often as you need. At the end of the day, reflect on how well you did being Engaging, Empowering, and Encouraging. Doing this day in and day out, it will soon become a habit for you.

.

7 Principles Checklist

Principle 1—Own The Plan
- o Know The Plan
- o Start Using It Immediately
- o Review Your Plan Regularly

Principle 2—Own The Culture
- o Human Resources Activities
- o Encourage Storytelling
- o Formal Speeches and Informal Chats
- o Recognize and Reward Employees

Principle 3—Stay Focused on What Matters Most
- o Make Sure Everyone Understands Their Ladder

Principle 4—Fanatical Focus on Next Quarter
- o Quarterly Visions
- o Everyone Knows Their Top 3
- o Defend Their Time and Attention
- o Keep it To One-Page

Principle 5—Empower Employees to be Responsive Decision Makers
- o Involve Employees in the Goal Setting
- o Give People a Framework to Be Owners
- o Ask a lot of Questions
- o Start Small and Be Patient

Principle 6—Remove Obstacles
- o Review and Revise Current Procedures and rules

Principle 7—Use Engage, Empower, and Encourage Approach

End Notes

1. 2013 State of the American Workplace. Gallup. http://www.gallup.com/strategicconsulting/163007/state-american-workplace.aspx

2. *The Office of Strategy Management,* by Robert Kaplan and David Norton, Harvard Business Review, Oct. 2005. http://hbr.org/2005/10/the-office-of-strategy-management/ar/1

3. James C. Collins and Jerry I. Porras, "Building Your Company's Vision," Harvard Business Review, Sept.–Oct. 1996.

4. Jerome Bruner, as cited by Paul Martin Lester in "Syntactic Theory of Visual Communication" http://blog.kareldonk.com/wp-content/uploads/2015/03/SyntacticTheoryofVisualCommunication.pdf

5. *Why Good Strategies Fail,* Economist special report, 2013. http://www.pmi.org/~/media/PDF/Publications/WhyGoodStrategiesFail_Report_EIU_PMI.ashx

6. Source: https://www.atlassian.com/time-wasting-at-work-infographic

7. How Much Information, by Roger E. Bohn and James E. Short. December 2009. UCSD. http://hmi.ucsd.edu/howmuchinfo_research_report_consum.php

Acknowledgments

I have a few people to thank. First, I would like to thank my parents Helane and Wilfried Koehler who taught me life lessons on how to treat others and how to persevere through adversity if you really want something. Growing up, I watched first-hand how they balanced raising a family and running their own successful small business.

Thank you to my wife Heidi and children Anja, Liesel, and Sophie. I am blessed to be given the title of husband and father, which has taught me how to be a better human being. Thank you for your patience as I continue to learn!

I need to thank the United States Navy for giving me the opportunity to learn how to be a leader of men in stressful situations. At 24 years of age, I was responsible for the safe operation of a $1B submarine and the lives of the 120-man crew on missions critical to national security.

Thanks to Peter Noland, Jeff Wohlwend, and Mark Pender who delivered on their promise that I would learn more actually running a small business than going back to school for an MBA.

Thanks to Pamela Wasley, Maria Hillman, and Kristin McAlister from Cerius Interim who put their faith in me to help turn around many distressed, small family run businesses.

Thanks to Gregg Schneider (President, Caseworx), Heather Finlay (CEO, YWCA of San Diego), and Bobbe Monteleone (President, Calmont)for letting me share their experience using *Leading With Purpose*.

Thank you to John Bertagnolli, my business partner. He is a technology guru who has brought the step-by-step process online so it is intuitive and easy for you to manage.

Thanks to Len Bertagnolli for proofing the content of this book. Your recommendations and edits helped increase its readability.

I am deeply grateful to my editor Rick Benzel for his help in putting this book into good shape, and to my book and cover designer Susan Shankin who artfully created this attractive book. Their company Over And Above Creative Group has done just exactly that—gone over and above in their commitment to help me publish this book in the most professional way possible.

About the Author

Marc Koehler is the President of Lead with Purpose, a company dedicated to helping people lead more purposeful lives. He brings over 30 years of business and life experiences that include US Navy Submarine Officer, Interim CEO/COO, Entrepreneur, Husband, Father, and Soccer Coach.

During the last ten years, Marc was brought into distressed companies as an interim CEO/COO. He developed a reputation as someone who could tackle the worst business situations. Marc led many companies on the verge of going under back to profitability. It was during this time that Marc witnessed the power of the human spirit and the role of a leader to inspire and help everyone reach their full potential.

He has four-year degrees in both Physics and Mechanical Engineering and is a Lean Six Sigma Black Belt. He served his country in the US Navy Submarine force from 1988 to 1993.

Marc is on the speaker's bureau of several well-known national executive and life coaching organizations. He is a sought after speaker and has been all over the United States spreading his message about leading a more purposeful life.

Marc is available for speeches and workshops at companies, business conferences, and other venues. For details, he can be reached at SpeakerInquiry@LeadWithPurpose.com.

Free Test Drive at www.LeadWithPurpose.com

We hope you have enjoyed reading this book and are eager to implement your own one-page plan and the principles in this book in your company.

We invite you for a free test drive of our online platform at www.LeadWithPurpose.com. If you like it, our monthly fees to continue using it are reasonable and affordable. If it can cost up to $15,000 to hire an outside strategic consultant to help you put a plan together, you could buy about 20 years of our online service. We are absolutely confident that you will find the Lead With Purpose platform to be a tremendous boost to your company. Do not hesitate to contact Marc@LeadWithPurpose.com with any questions you have about our website.

***

Lead With Purpose Coaching Certification

If you are an executive coach, life coach, or consultant and you are interested in using Lead With Purpose to help your clients lead more purposeful and inspiring lives, you can become a Lead With Purpose Certified Coach. Go to www.LeadWithPurpose.com to learn more.

Milton Keynes UK
Ingram Content Group UK Ltd.
UKHW052024230524
442964UK00003B/7